SHE SWEEPS HER DIRT

Having A Grateful Heart

TRACY ADAMS

Dedication

To my grandchildren, Liam and Danni,
always follow Jesus and have a grateful heart.
Sweep your dirt every day.

Table of Contents

Introduction

In 2005, my daughter, close friends, church family, and I journeyed to South Africa on a mission trip. After the long eighteen-hour flight to Johannesburg, we boarded a bus for a four-hour journey to White River. Exhausted but excited to be in South Africa to start our mission, I anxiously gazed out the window, taking in the sights of this foreign land. As we traveled, we quickly rode past small villages where some of the homes were made up of only single rooms with slated walls filled with rocks and mud. These homes generally had a single door and window with, at times, a mere cloth covering the openings. The meager homes had dirt floors and metal roofs, typically held down with large rocks.

As sadness filled my heart at how some of the people lived, I saw what I thought was most unusual. A woman stood outside her small home in a long dress, her hair wrapped with a scarf, holding a handmade broom. It was a long, sturdy stick with what appeared to be straw tied to one end with twine. She was sweeping the dirt outside her home. While in South Africa, I encountered many things that were unlike anything I had ever experienced or seen before, but this image has forever remained etched in my mind. Although a fleeting moment, I'll never forget it. At the time, I didn't realize that God would repeatedly bring that moment back to me. Over time, He would show me what that beautiful woman had. Something that, unfortunately, many of us do not. Something that money cannot buy.

Although she had very little regarding material possessions, she worked diligently to improve what she possessed. Yes, she had dirt, but she had clean dirt! What causes one to do something such as that? What causes someone to appreciate and care for what they have, even when it's very little? One word—gratitude.

PART ONE

RECEIVE GOD'S BLESSINGS

Don't focus on what you don't have;
focus on what you do have

CHAPTER 1

From the Heart

A grateful heart and thankfulness will improve your life on Earth. God's word says so much about thankfulness. In this book, I have referenced Scripture to show what God says about being thankful, but for now, I want to speak from the heart.

We are on this Earth until God decides to call us home. We can choose to spend our earthly days following Him and be grateful for all He does for us, or we can choose to grumble, complain, and act like a victim. I am so incredibly blessed. Was I born into a wealthy family? In the worldly sense, no. However, I was born into a wealthy family in the godly sense; I was born into a godly family that taught me about Jesus. I learned about God's goodness. In a working-class family, I learned that we worked for what we had and were not entitled to anything we didn't work for. I learned that things are not free, and someone always pays the price. I learned to give others a helping hand. I learned to be generous. I learned to be respectful and polite. I learned about Jesus.

There were years of my life when I didn't see the goodness of God. His goodness was there; I just didn't *see* it. I didn't recognize it because I wasn't looking. I lived part of my life thinking, "Life isn't fair." I had many pity parties asking, "Why me?" The reality is, life isn't fair; Satan runs amuck in this world. I lived part of my life focusing on all I didn't have instead of all I did have. I lived part of my life not following Jesus. It's not that I didn't believe in Him or that I wasn't saved, but I wasn't actively following Him.

Jesus was my Savior, but there was a time when He was not my Shepherd. Jesus Christ becomes our Savior when we know in our hearts that He is the only way to God. When we acknowledge that He is the living Son of God, born of a virgin, who, although He was sinless, died a sinner's death on a cross to pay for the sins of the world. Jesus died, was buried, and rose to life after three days. Once we trust Jesus Christ as our Savior, we will spend eternity in Heaven with Him. However, if Jesus is our Shepherd, we have a relationship with Him, and if we truly love Him, we follow His commands. We follow His ways, not society's ways. When Jesus is our Shepherd, we can experience and bring a little bit of Heaven down to Earth.

Life is hard. It's especially hard when you live life without Jesus. When Jesus was not my Shepherd, there was no peace in my soul. I could not pinpoint what was wrong, but I was not at peace. What does a lack of peace bring? Sleepless nights, health issues, worry, anxiety, and more.

Following Jesus can be difficult from an earthly, worldly standpoint. Society glorifies and seems to reward bad behavior,

behavior that violates God's word. When you stand with God, you will be in the minority. Remember, we can only please God or man, not both. In Isaiah 7:9, God says, "'If you don't stand firm in your faith, you will not stand at all'" (NIV). Know what you believe in and why you believe it, and grow your roots deep. Then, when trials and temptations come along (and they will), you can stand firm. Standing against the crowd is hard. That is why you need to grow your relationship with Jesus so that you know Him and realize that you never stand alone. Know His character, know His promises, and know His faithfulness.

As I matured in Christ, Jesus became my Shepherd. I decided I would follow Him completely. Life has not been perfect since then; no life is. But I have peace in my soul. I go to bed at night with a clear conscience. I fail Him daily, but I know He forgives me daily, and I strive to act according to His will the next day.

I am so thankful for all that God gives me. I am incredibly grateful for His grace and mercy. He generously gives me both.

Don't focus on what you don't have; focus on what you do have. Always search for the good. Wake up each morning with a grateful heart, and you will have a smile on your face. No matter how bad things are, something good is always waiting to be found. God is all around us. Recognize Him, seek Him, and thank Him!

Having a heart of thankfulness and gratitude will bring you joy. People will look at you and want what you have. People will want to be around you. People like being around those who are upbeat and positive. It's miserable to be around someone who is always negative. They drain the energy right out of you.

It's incredible how you can change someone's day with a smile or a positive word. Build people up and encourage them. Fill baskets; don't tip them over. Even if you don't know someone, you can make a difference in their day. I cannot tell you the number of times I have spoken something positive and kind to someone I didn't even know, someone I just encountered, and they said, "Wow, I needed that. Thank you." Will you always get that kind of response? No, but most people appreciate a smile and a kind word.

So, how can you naturally be positive? By being thankful. As you grow closer to God, developing your relationship with Him, you will become more grateful.

I hope this book will help you learn more about our God and our Savior, Jesus Christ. I hope He will become your Shepherd, and you will choose to wholeheartedly follow Him. Now, let's dig into God's word together!

Truth is the absolute standard
by which reality is measured

CHAPTER 2

God's Blessing

As Christians, we often hear the word "blessing." The question to answer is, "What is a blessing?" Simply put, it's a gift from God, the goodness of God in our lives. There are countless ways in which God blesses us. Firstly, He blesses us by providing us with a pathway to spend eternity with Him through His Son, Jesus Christ. On this side of Heaven, God blesses us by allowing us to go directly to Him and have a personal relationship. Moreover, He blesses us with His grace, mercy, providence, and protection. Above all, God blesses us by loving us unconditionally.

It's important to recognize and acknowledge God, have a relationship with Him, and show appreciation and gratitude to Him. We will take a deep dive and dissect how our relationship is formed with God and how we are to show gratitude to Him through worship. We will examine what God says about receiving His blessings.

Relationship

How can we express our appreciation and gratitude to God for all He has blessed us with? One way is to simply thank Him.

Why do we need to thank God? There are a multitude of reasons why we should show our gratitude to God. Firstly, God gives us everything we possess. We possess nothing under the sun—be it our health, desires, family, friends, job, mental capacity, and yes, our physical possessions—that isn't given to us by God. The list is endless. However, the most important reason to thank God is because God's written word commands us to do so:

> In every thing give thanks: for this is the will of God in Christ Jesus concerning you (1 Thessalonians 5:18, KJV).

> And give thanks for everything to God the Father in the name of our Lord Jesus Christ (Ephesians 5:20, NLT).

What compels us to give thanks to God? Simply put—relationship. Without a relationship with God, it most likely does not cross our minds to thank Him. When we have a close relationship with someone, we want to do things that please them and often think about them. We show appreciation by spending time with them, speaking of them favorably to others, and doing things for them. We know their heart and their character. In turn, they also know ours.

A relationship is needed with God for us to give thanks from the heart—true, sincere thanks. The following section will take a deep dive; it's crucial to understand man's being and the formation of the relationship with God. Here we go!

The Make-Up of Man

Let's start by answering the question, "What are we?" There are two general views on the make-up of man.[a] One view is that man is a dichotomy comprising two parts—body and soul, with the soul containing the spirit. The other view is that man is a trichotomy comprising three parts—body, soul, and spirit.[b]

Whether you believe in dichotomy or trichotomy, all three—body, soul, and spirit—are addressed throughout the Bible. We will examine each.

In 1 Thessalonians, Paul distinguishes three components of man:

> Now may the God of peace make you holy
> in every way, and may your whole spirit and
> soul and body be kept blameless until our Lord
> Jesus Christ comes again
> (1 Thessalonians 5:23, NLT).

Natural man only has two of these three parts—body and soul. We know that the body is physical. We will look at the soul and address the spirit in the next section.

> And the LORD God formed man of the dust of
> the ground, and breathed into his nostrils the

21

breath of life; and man became a living soul (Genesis 2:7 KJV).

The word "soul" is translated from the Hebrew word *nephesh,* which means:

A breathing creature, i.e., animal, or man's inner being.

Your soul is who you are, your personality. The soul is nothing more and nothing less than what gives a body life. The soul is not spirit and has nothing to do with whether you are a Christian. Once someone is breathing and living, they have a soul.

An interesting note is the first four times the Hebrew Bible uses the word *nephesh* it refers to animals: sea life (Genesis 1:20), great sea life (Genesis 1:21), land creatures (Genesis 1:24), and birds and land creatures (Genesis 1:30).

Genesis 1:30 says that all living things have a soul. Then, in Genesis 2:7, *nephesh* describes man, "Man became a living soul" (KJV).

Worship God

Genesis tells us about the creation of man:

So God created mankind in his own image, in the image of God he created them; male and female he created them (Genesis 1:27, NIV).

God created mankind in His own image. So, the obvious question is, "What is God's image?" Jesus tells us:

> "For God is Spirit, so those who worship him
> must worship in spirit and in truth."
> (John 4:24, NLT).

God's image is Spirit. There is a lot in this passage, and we will break it down piece by piece. First is the word "worship." The word "worship" is translated from the Greek word *proskuneó*, which means:

> To do reverence to.

Worshipping God requires us to revere Him and place our full attention on Him. In the truest sense of worship, there are no distractions that take our focus off of Him. There are many ways to worship, such as through song, prayer, praise, thanksgiving, reading, and studying His word.

Jesus tells us that there are two necessary components for worshiping God. Jesus tells us that we must worship God in spirit and in truth.

1. Spirit

God is a Spirit, so one must worship in Spirit to worship God. We can only worship through the Holy Spirit and must worship with the right heart, the right motivation.

Now, we get to the third component of man's being: spirit. Each of us is born with a dormant spirit. However, when we accept Jesus Christ as our personal Lord and Savior, our spirit is activated, and we are immediately saved and will spend eternity in Heaven. The Holy Spirit comes and dwells within us. When Jesus spoke to His disciples before His crucifixion, He told them of the Holy Spirit:

> "Then I will ask the Father to send you the Holy Spirit who will help you and always be with you. The Spirit will show you what is true. The people of this world cannot accept the Spirit, because they don't see or know him. But you know the Spirit, who is with you and will keep on living in you"
> (John 14:16-17, CEV).

> "But I tell you that I am going to do what is best for you. That is why I am going away. The Holy Spirit cannot come to help you until I leave. But after I am gone, I will send the Spirit to you" (John 16:7, CEV).

The word "spirit" is translated from the Greek word *pneuma* and refers to how God communicates the knowledge of truth to man through the Holy Spirit. Our spirit releases life into our soul; our soul releases life into our body. Our spirit exists because of God and for our relationship with God. Our soul is naturally worldly and self-centered. Worldliness is living life our way, according to culture, not according to God's word. Basically, it's leaving Him out of our decisions and how we act and behave.

2. Truth

For the soul to act according to the spirit, the soul must agree with the spirit; this is where truth comes in. In today's world, the definition of truth is blurred and confusing. There are two overarching ways to view truth. One is from a worldly perspective, and the other is from God's perspective.[c]

Worldly Perspective:

1. Relativism: Relativism is the way "I see it." Since this is how "I see it," it must be reality, and I may see it differently tomorrow. With relativism, truth can always change.

2. Post-Modernism: Post-modernism is what "I want it to be." I have the way I want it to be in my mind, so it is true. This is commonly known as "my truth." "My truth" is constantly redefined based on my emotions, feelings, or circumstances.

The "truths" of relativism and post-modernism are subjective, can change, and cause much confusion. When this thinking is presented or pushed on others, people don't know what is true, what they can believe, or who they can believe, leaving many unanswered questions.

God's Perspective:

What is an accurate definition of truth?

> Truth is an absolute standard by which reality is measured.[d]

Truth is objective and transcends emotions. We need to understand that truth exists and is knowable. Jesus tells us we will know the truth and the truth will set us free (John 8:32).

Truth does not confuse. Truth sets you free. When I was young, I never really understood what Jesus said about truth setting us free. As I've grown older, I've realized that making wise and educated decisions requires knowing the absolute truth. Without it, we can easily make unwise decisions and choose the wrong path.

Referring back to John 4:24, Jesus tells us that we "'must worship in spirit and in truth.'" For the spirit to feed into the soul, the soul must agree with the spirit. That is why we must start with truth. The Holy Spirit that resides within us can *only* take in the truth; truth corresponds to the nature and will of God.

Truth is rooted in God—not in culture, not in history, not in our background. From a biblical perspective, truth is God's point of view on any subject.

Knowing God's truth is incredibly important; know the difference between facts and truth. Facts don't always equate to truth; ponder on that statement. The story of the Israelites and the Promised Land illustrates how facts can get in the way of God's truth. In Numbers 13:1, God told Moses that He was giving the Israelites the land of Canaan. By God's instruction, each of the twelve tribes sent a spy to explore the land. However, ten of the spies were blinded by the facts and overlooked God's truth. The spies reported that the people living in the Promised Land were powerful, some were giants, and their cities were large and fortified (Numbers 13:28). The ten said, "We can't go up against them! They are stronger than we are!" (Numbers 13:31). The Israelites allowed the facts to overpower the truth that God had revealed to them. God had promised them that the land was theirs. If they had listened to God's truth and obeyed Him, they would have avoided spending forty years in the wilderness. Rest in God's truth.

On a lighter note, there's a story about a man who told his wife he was going fishing. After several hours on the lake, he had caught nothing. Because of his pride and embarrassment over not catching any fish, he went to the local fish market. He asked the vendor to toss a fish to him. The vendor tossed the fish, and the man caught it. He then went home and told his wife, "See the big fish I caught?" He didn't lie, but he led her to believe something untrue. Yes, he technically caught the fish, but not in the way he knew she would assume he had; he presented a fact but didn't present the truth.

If the definition of truth is an absolute standard by which reality is measured, what is our absolute standard as Christians? God. God's view on any matter. God is the creator of all things; He is the source of all truth, and His view never changes. Both the Old and New Testaments tell us that God never changes:

> Jesus Christ is the same yesterday, today, and forever (Hebrews 13:8, NLT).

> "I the LORD do not change" (Malachi 3:6, NIV).

> Every good and perfect gift is from above, coming down from the Father of the heavenly

lights, who does not change like shifting shadows (James 1:17, NIV).

God is the same yesterday, today, and tomorrow. God does not change with society or the world, unlike "my truth," which constantly changes with my current emotions, circumstances, and time.

There is only one truth. Know the truth of God by spending time with Him, developing a relationship through prayer, and reading and studying His written word. I take great comfort in the fact that God never changes. We can learn about God's character, His promises, and the fulfillment of His promises in the Bible and know in our hearts that His words still hold true today.

Worship God in spirit and in truth. As Christians, we possess the Holy Spirit. We need to let the Holy Spirit be the leader of our lives as we worship God in His truth, the truth He has given us.

Blessings

As we worship and acknowledge God for all He has done for us, we build and strengthen our relationship with Him. Jesus tells us what happens as we walk closely with Him. In a nutshell, we will receive God's blessings:

> "If you abide in Me, and My words abide in you, you will ask what you desire, and it shall be done for you" (John 15:7, KJV).

Let's break this passage down. I don't want you to read this and think it isn't true because maybe God didn't give you what you asked for. What does Jesus mean when He says, "'You will ask what you desire, and it shall be done for you'"? We have all asked for things that God didn't give us. Why have we not received all that we have asked for? If we truly abide in God and His word, then His desires will become our desires. God will only give according to His desires. So, when our desires change from worldly desires and align with His, it shall be done. One of my favorite passages is in Psalms, and it too speaks to this truth:

> Delight yourself in the LORD;
> And He will give you the desires of your heart
> (Psalm 37:4, NASB).

Know God's word, know His promises, know His goodness, and know His nature. As we grow closer to God, we see more and more of His beauty and glory; we recognize that all things in our lives are from Him. God pours blessings upon us daily; the problem is that we don't always recognize them.

Remember, a blessing is the goodness of God in our lives. We have the capacity to enjoy God's goodness when we recognize the things God has done in our lives. God blesses us with many gifts, big and small; God smiles upon us daily. The more we see and recognize His blessings (His favor), the more we show our thankfulness and the more we see His blessings. It becomes a circle. Within this circle is the peace of God within our souls.

> Don't worry about anything; instead, pray
> about everything. Tell God what you need,

and thank him for all he has done. Then you will experience God's peace, which exceeds anything we can understand. His peace will guard your hearts and minds as you live in Christ Jesus (Philippians 4:6-7, NLT).

For me, God's peace is a huge blessing. Whenever things are not going as I would like, I am genuinely thankful when there is a calm within my soul. I immediately know where that calm is coming from—not from me. When we experience chaos and turmoil, we can still experience God's peace within our souls.

Remain in God's Word

Final thought: If we want to know God, His character, and His promises, we must be in His word. The Bible teaches us wisdom. The Bible shows us how God views His creation. God's word is living; it applies to us today. Focus on God and strive to please Him.

Grounding ourselves in God's word also gives us hope and encouragement when Satan attacks us. God's word needs to be in our hearts so that when stress, anxiety, doubt, fear, temptation, heartache, and heartbreak come into our lives, we are ready to fall back on God's word and promises. In Ephesians, Paul tells us to put on the armor of God. However, for the Christian in battle, he only recommends one weapon of attack—the sword of the Spirit (Ephesians 6:13-17), which is the word of God. Know God's word!

How does all this tie together? When we come to know and put our faith in Jesus Christ, the Holy Spirit is activated and indwells us. We can now directly communicate with God through the Holy Spirit. The Holy Spirit feeds into our souls, which feeds into our bodies. Once the Holy Spirit abides in us, and as we abide in God's written word, we come to know God's truth more and more, building our relationships with Him. As our relationships build, our desires begin to align with His desires. We then see God's blessings upon our lives more and more. As we see and recognize our blessings, we naturally thank God for them. Always remain in God's word to continually grow your relationship with Him, finding strength and encouragement.

Faith is trusting that God will do
what He says He will do

CHAPTER 3

Answered Prayers

Another way that God blesses us is with answered prayers. When we pray, answers to our prayers reside in the spiritual realm, although not yet received here on Earth.[a] In Daniel 9, we see Daniel reading the word written by Jeremiah and praying to God for its meaning. In Daniel 10, Daniel receives his answer, but only after twenty-one days have elapsed.

> Then he said, "Don't be afraid, Daniel. Since the first day you began to pray for understanding and to humble yourself before your God, your request has been heard in heaven. I have come in answer to your prayer. But for twenty-one days the spirit prince of the kingdom of Persia blocked my way. Then Michael, one of the archangels, came to help me, and I left him there with the spirit prince of the kingdom of Persia. Now I am here to explain what will

happen to your people in the future, for this
vision concerns a time yet to come"
(Daniel 10: 12-14, NLT).

During prayer, thank God for the answers already given, although not yet received. Thank Him for what He has already done and what He is currently working out. Draw out the answer with prayer and thanksgiving. An acorn contains a mighty oak tree; it just has to be drawn out by planting it in the ground and giving it water to grow. The same is true with prayers; all answers to prayers reside in the spiritual realm. We must draw them out through prayer and a relationship with our Father.

Does God deliver the answer to all our prayers according to our timetable? No, He answers them and delivers them according to His timetable, which may or may not align with ours. However, it's important to remember that we are responsible for praying for the answers we seek. One day, when we get to Heaven, we will realize all the blessings God would have given us if we had only asked.

> "Keep on asking, and you will receive what
> you ask for. Keep on seeking, and you will
> find. Keep on knocking, and the door will be
> opened to you" (Matthew 7:7, NLT).

Does God always answer our prayers in the way we have asked? No. Remember, what we ask for has to align with His will.

Will we always see God's answer? Not necessarily on this side of Heaven. Just know that no matter what is going on in your life, God is always at work, and you may or may not see it. This is where faith comes in. What is faith? The writer of Hebrews tells us it is confidence in what we hope for and assurance in what we do not see (Hebrews 11:1). Simply put, faith is trusting that God will do what He says He will do.

Be thankful for our sovereign God, who controls all things and allows nothing to happen that does not first pass through His hands.

Share and Give Thanks

Share your thanksgivings and received blessings with others. Psalms tells us to sing a song of thanksgiving and tell of all God's wonders (Psalm 26:7). When we give thanks and tell of God's greatness, we glorify Him.

Share what God has done in your life with others. Doing this gives others hope. Let others see how God is working in your life. Sharing your thanksgivings will help others ponder and think about what God is doing in their own lives. Bring awareness to all that He does. I find it exciting and encouraging when someone shares how God has blessed them or performed a miracle in their lives.

As a parent, think about how you want to bless your children—by loving them, spending time with them, and creating those special memories. How wonderful does it feel when your child acknowledges what you have done and thanks you? How much does it mean to hear your child share about the time they spent with you with one of their friends? Similarly, God also appreciates it when His children acknowledge Him, thank Him, and share His goodness with others.

Sometimes, God blesses us out of His goodness, but when we thank Him, the blessing becomes greater. Luke tells us the story of the ten men who had leprosy:

> Now it happened as He went to Jerusalem that He passed through the midst of Samaria and Galilee. Then as He entered a certain village, there met Him ten men who were lepers, who stood afar off. And they lifted up their voices and said, "Jesus, Master, have mercy on us!"
>
> So when He saw them, He said to them, "Go, show yourselves to the priests." And so it was that as they went, they were cleansed.
>
> And one of them, when he saw that he was healed, returned, and with a loud voice glorified God, and fell down on his face at His feet, giving Him thanks. And he was a Samaritan.
>
> So Jesus answered and said, "Were there not ten cleansed? But where are the nine? Were there not any found who returned to give glory to God except this foreigner?" And He said to him, "Arise, go your way. Your faith has made you well" (Luke 17:11-19, NKJV).

In biblical times, when someone had leprosy, they were cast out of their camp or city and were segregated into colonies.

People believed that God was punishing individuals who had leprosy. In ancient times, there was no medical cure for leprosy. Lepers were considered socially, religiously, and physically unclean. From the book of Leviticus, if a person with a skin disease was healed, they were required to present themselves to the priest for inspection and ceremonial purification.

In verse 13, the men, standing at a distance, called out to Jesus, "'Jesus, Master.'" The word "Master" in this particular verse is translated from the Greek word *epistates* and appears only seven times in the New Testament (Luke 5:5; Luke 8:24 (twice); Luke 8:45; Luke 9:33; Luke 9:49; Luke 17:13). Jesus' disciples used it in the other six instances. The Greek word *epistates* means:

> A master, the one fully authorized, the head (owner) of all things.

The lepers recognized Jesus' authority. When the ten followed Jesus' direction to go show themselves to the priest, as God's people were told to do in Leviticus, they were cleansed of their leprosy. As they went, they were cleansed, so they demonstrated faith. They were not cleansed and then went—they went, and then they were cleansed.

Only one of the ten lepers came back, a Samaritan. He "returned, and with a loud voice glorified God, and fell down on his face at His feet, giving Him thanks" (Luke 17:15-16, NKJV). Only one glorified God and gave thanks to Jesus. Not only did he give thanks, he threw himself at Jesus' feet. The one saw Jesus for who He was, recognized the tremendous blessing he had received, rejoiced, loudly praised, and glorified God. He did this openly and publicly.

In verse 18, Jesus recognized that only one "'returned to give glory to God.'" The word "glory" is translated from the Greek word *doxa* and, in this particular passage, means:

> Declaring one's gratitude to God for a benefit received.

Indeed, the one received a significant physical benefit when he was healed from leprosy!

So now, here comes the good part—verse 19. Jesus says, "'Rise and go; your faith has made you well.'" The word "well" is translated from the Greek word *sózó*, which means:

> God rescuing believers from the penalty and power of sin.

God saved the one! The one was cleansed not only on the outside but also on the inside. The other nine only got their skin cleaned; the one received the spiritual blessing of salvation.

Why is it that God blesses us when we are grateful? Because God wants us to recognize Him and to show Him appreciation.

Be the ONE! Recognize what God has done for you and thank Him.

Be Specific

Always remember to thank God for answered prayers. I have prayed for sick family members, for my children and grandchildren, for pending surgeries, and for jobs, as I am sure you have too. When God answers those prayers, remember to go back and thank Him. Pray for safe travels and protection of your home when you are away. Thank Him when you return safely and all is well with your home. Tell God your needs, your desires. Yes, He already knows in advance what you need, but acknowledge it to Him. When praying, don't pray vaguely; be specific so that when your prayer is answered, you see God's hand.

Thank God in advance of receiving. In Matthew, there are two accounts where Jesus preaches to the multitudes and provides food for them. In Matthew 14:13-21, Jesus takes five loaves of bread and two fish and feeds 5,000 (plus the women and children). In Matthew 15:32-39, Jesus takes seven loaves of bread and a few small fish and feeds 4,000 (plus the women and children). In both cases, Jesus fed everyone until they were satisfied, and there were leftovers. Both of these accounts are miracles, no doubt. Before distributing the food, Jesus gave thanks to God for the food. There was only physically enough food in both accounts for a few people at best. He thanked God for the provision, a provision that appeared not to be enough. Sometimes, we have to give thanks in faith, saying, "I'm going to trust you and give thanks in advance for what I trust you are going to do." Thank Him for what He is going to do.

This concept seems backward. Typically, we pray to God for something we need or desire, and once God answers, we thank Him. In the passages where Jesus feeds the multitudes, Jesus demonstrates praying to God, thanking Him in advance for His answer, and then waiting and seeing His blessing.

Prayer strengthens our relationship with God. Prayer does not have to be elegant or formal; talk to Him as you would with a close friend. Be specific in your prayers, and don't use general terms. Instead of saying, "Lord, bless me today," ask for specific blessings you desire. For example, "Lord, please keep me safe as I commute to and from work," or "Lord, help me think clearly and recall what I have learned as I take my exam today." When dealing with a difficult conversation or situation, ask for guidance and the right words to say. When someone you know is struggling, ask for God's help and comfort on their behalf. Speak to God from your heart and thank Him in advance of receiving. Here is a prayer that I frequently prayed for my daughter when she was a child: "God, I pray blessings and protection upon Taylor's future husband; thank you that he is in a home that teaches him about Jesus. Please provide him with your protection." There have been occasions in my life when I was so distraught all I could say was, "Holy Spirit, please pray for me; please go to God on my behalf; I am not able." Yes, prayers can be cries from the heart.

PART TWO

AVOID THE BARRIERS TO A GRATEFUL HEART

Never let wealth become riches
in your life

Foolishness and wisdom
are not intellectual issues;
they are moral issues

You are in control of concern;
worry is in control of you

CHAPTER 4

Barriers to Gratitude

We will look at gratitude and the barriers that keep us from being grateful. My hope is you will self-reflect on these barriers and avoid them in your life.

As we develop and grow our relationship with Christ Jesus, Paul tells us in Colossians what will happen:

> And now, just as you accepted Christ Jesus as your Lord, you must continue to follow him. Let your roots grow down into him, and let your lives be built on him. Then your faith will grow strong in the truth you were taught, and you will overflow with thankfulness (Colossians 2:6-7, NLT).

We will "overflow with thankfulness."

Paul tells us to grow our roots deep by building our lives on Jesus. As we do this, we will naturally overflow with thankfulness. When my daughter was young, I used to impress upon her to grow her roots deep and know what and whom she believed in and why. Growing your roots deep helps you stand strong against things you know are wrong. Seemingly little things, like growing our roots deep, can significantly impact our lives. It's essential to instill this life-changing principle in our children and grandchildren.

Thanking God seems so simple. Yet, we tend to forget. What keeps us from thanking God? What is it in life that causes us to "forget" to see God and thank Him? Here are four barriers to thankfulness that can get in our way.[a]

1. Materialism

Materialism is a tendency to consider material possessions and physical comfort more important than spiritual values. It's a belief that money can satisfy. So, what does the richest person who ever lived say about materialism? In Ecclesiastes, Solomon, the wisest, richest king, wrote:

> He who loves silver will not be satisfied with silver; Nor he who loves abundance, with increase. This also is vanity
> (Ecclesiastes 5:10, NKJV).

The word "vanity" is translated from the Hebrew word *hebel*, which means:

Emptiness or something unsatisfactory.

Solomon uses this word thirty-eight times in the book of Ecclesiastes. As Solomon looked about his vast riches and fortune, he realized it was full of emptiness. The man who had it all regarding earthly riches and possessions was left empty. Even though God gave Solomon wisdom, Solomon let his wealth become riches.

It's okay to have wealth; it isn't a sin to be wealthy. The problem isn't with wealth; the problem is with your priority. Is God first in your life or is money? If you focus on money, materialism, and riches, there will be little room for God. Solomon began to take part in worshiping false gods, the gods of his many wives. Solomon didn't keep the one true God as his focus and priority.

There is a spiritual distinction between wealth and riches, and the distinction lies in the attitude of the heart. On Earth, someone who loves riches has the attitude of a self-indulgent heart, "I want more; there is never enough." On the other hand, wealthy people see their wealth as a gift from God; they view their wealth as belonging to God. They believe He has entrusted them with it to use in ways that honor and glorify Him. Many translations of the Bible use the words "wealth" and "riches" interchangeably. However, it's essential to note that these words can be good or bad, depending on the heart and priority. Riches are merely money and material possessions, with God not being the priority. Wealth encompasses so much more. Wealth involves things that money cannot buy. However, wealth can include material possessions as long as God remains the priority.

Don't let this be confusing. There is a passage in the Bible that we'll talk about later that speaks about "true riches." When the Bible speaks of "true riches," it's talking about spiritual blessings. Remember from Chapter 2, truth in the Bible is God's truth.

As a child growing up, my family wasn't rich in the eyes of the world. There were many struggles, although I was unaware of them as a child. When I was in first grade with thirty-one other children, I was the only one whose mommy had to work to help make ends meet. We were not rich, but oh, we were wealthy. All the money in the world could never replace the home I was raised in, a home full of love and security.

If we get wrapped up in materialism, always wanting more, we will forget God. Never let wealth become riches in your life. If this happens, spiritual growth and thanking God for the blessings He gives will cease to exist. Moses reminds us of where our abilities come from:

> "But remember the LORD your God, for it is he
> who gives you the ability to produce wealth,
> and so confirms his covenant, which he swore
> to your ancestors, as it is today"
> (Deuteronomy 8:18, NIV).

Remember, God gives us the ability to learn, grow, and have opportunities. He gives us wisdom and understanding. Without these things, how can one ever begin to obtain wealth? Yes, we work hard in life, but God gives us the ability and the desire. If you have a unique talent or skill—artist, bricklayer, electrician—God gave you those talents and skills. If you have a college degree, God gave you the ability and opportunity to obtain that degree. If you have a great job, God gave you that opportunity. If you are in good health and have a loving family, that, too, is the fruit of God's blessings.

In Mark, when Jesus told the Parable of the Sower, He had this to say about riches:

> "…and the cares of this world, the deceitfulness of riches, and the desires for other things entering in choke the word, and it becomes unfruitful" (Mark 4:19, NKJV).

In this passage, "riches" is translated from the Greek word *ploutos,* which means:

Abundance of external possessions.

Jesus clearly states that riches are deceitful. Riches are deceitful in making you think they are more than what they are and can give. Satan tries to deceive us into believing that material riches hold the key to our happiness and the fulfillment of our desires. The measure of living well isn't riches; money and riches cannot buy love, inner peace, joy, or eternity in Heaven with our Lord. Paul explains so well in just two short verses what running after riches will cause:

> Those who want to get rich fall into temptation and a trap and into many foolish and harmful desires that plunge people into ruin and destruction. For the love of money is a root of all kinds of evil. Some people, eager for money, have wandered from the faith and pierced themselves with many griefs (1 Timothy 6:9-10, NIV).

I want to emphasize again that having material wealth isn't a sin. Having and obtaining wealth is okay as long as God is always first and leads your journey. Include God in your personal relationships, jobs, financial pursuits, purchases, and giving to His kingdom. Never wander away from the faith and from God. If you do, as Paul puts it, you will pierce yourself with many griefs.

2. Comparison

I will briefly touch on this since the next chapter covers comparison in depth. God has a unique plan for each of our lives. When we compare ourselves to others, we quickly forget this.

> We do not dare to classify or compare ourselves with some who commend themselves. When they measure themselves by themselves and compare themselves with themselves, they are not wise (2 Corinthians 10:12, NIV).

Paul points out two things in this verse. First, don't compare yourself to others. Second, when people who praise themselves compare themselves to their own standards, they are not wise; some translations use the word "foolish."

The word "wise" is translated from the Greek word *suniémi*, which means:

> To "put facts together" and is closely connected with discerning and doing "the preferred will of God."

In Scripture, foolishness and wisdom are not intellectual issues; they are moral issues.[b]

Be discerning and strive to do the preferred will of God. Wisdom is how we use the knowledge we have obtained in life, and we need to use it according to God's word. Life on Earth is hard, but if we walk with God, being pleasing to Him, He will walk us through life's storms. Life is so much easier when we walk with our Heavenly Father.

One of my favorite quotes is by Eleanor Roosevelt:

> Never mistake knowledge for wisdom.
> One helps you make a living,
> the other helps you make a life.

Final note: Jesus Christ is the standard for comparison. We need to focus on Him and what God has for our lives and not concern ourselves with what God has for other people's lives. Give Him thanks for the things He has for you!

3. Pride

Let me briefly touch on this topic, as Chapter 7 covers pride in detail. Pride is a massive barrier to thankfulness. Pride is the belief that any and every good thing results from what we have done. It's no wonder God hates pride. Proverbs directly tell us that God hates pride:

> All who fear the LORD will hate evil.
>   Therefore, I hate pride and arrogance,
>   corruption and perverse speech
> (Proverbs 8:13, NLT).

What about arrogance? In essence, arrogance is pride in action. Pride shows the attitude that a person is independent of God. When someone lives in a way that does not recognize God for all He has done, they display arrogance by acting upon their pride. We act arrogantly when we elevate our thinking and reasoning above God. God hates pride and arrogance, and so should we.

Proverbs also tells us:

> Pride leads to disgrace,
>   but with humility comes wisdom
> (Proverbs 11:2, NLT).

The proud believes he is the master of his fate but fails to understand that pride goes before a fall. Humility is the recognition of yourself in relation to God. Remember, everything we have comes from God. We need to humble ourselves before God and exalt Him. With humility comes wisdom—knowing God's will and living life according to His plan.

God wants us to draw near to Him. We cannot give credit to God if we take credit for ourselves for all that we have. Hence, pride draws us away from God.

4. Busyness

We live in a busy world. There is so much to say about busyness.

The bottom line is that the busier we are, the quicker we forget about God. Satan loves when we are too busy, too busy for God. There is a saying, "If the devil can't make you sin, he'll make you busy." There is truth in this. When busy, we are distracted and try to do things in our own strength. The day comes and goes, and God doesn't even cross our minds. When we forget about Him, we don't see His hand at work, we don't see His blessings, we don't recognize Him, and sadly, we don't give Him the glory in our day. We don't thank Him.

Life can be incredibly hectic with working, going to school, doing homework, athletics, kids' activities, and caring for kids, elderly parents, and our home; the list is never-ending. When I was younger, I thought that once I graduated college, life would become less hectic, and I would have more free time. As I grew older, I believed that life would be less busy once my daughter graduated high school, and I would have more time to spare. Now that I'm much older, I realize that even the thought of retirement seems to hold the promise of a leisurely life with more free time. Technology was supposed to simplify our lives and give us back our time. However, as someone who grew up in a non-technical world and now lives in a world where technology is ubiquitous, I have found that life has become busier and more complex. The issue isn't with work, kids, elderly parents, school, or technology. Instead, the problem lies with us. Busyness isn't a virtue; it's often a vice. Let's examine God's word and see what He has to say.

Solomon reminds us in Psalms that it's the Lord who blesses our daily lives:

> It is vain for you to rise early,
> To retire late,
> To eat the bread of anxious labors—

51

> For He gives [blessings] to His beloved even in
> his sleep (Psalm 127:2, AMP).

God provides for our every need, even when we sleep! He is the One we should depend upon. When we separate our work from God and live our everyday lives in our strength, we eventually will see the futility and uselessness of it all. No matter how much we accomplish, there is always more work, and we will never feel satisfied. When we work independently from God, we discover that it's in vain to rise early and to retire late. Instead, the psalmist tells us what we should do:

> Be still, and know that I am God;
> I will be exalted among the nations,
> I will be exalted in the earth!
> (Psalm 46:10, NKJV).

Be still and know. What does that mean? Spend time with God, develop a relationship, and sit quietly with Him. By studying God's written word, we learn of God's character and who God is. We see His promises; we see His promises fulfilled. Stop, recognize, and truly understand from your heart that He is God. Sometimes, in all the craziness of our day and life, we need to stop, step back, close our eyes, and acknowledge who He is and what He can do. We need to stop trying to accomplish everything in our strength. We need to stop stressing out about our daily battles and trust God. God assures us that we have nothing to fear (Isaiah 41:10). He is with us. He will fight our battles, deal with our daily struggles, and conquer our enemies. Be patient, be still, and let Him go to work. If we don't trust and truly believe God is who He says He is, then it will be impossible to be still. Mother Teresa, a Catholic nun who served as a missionary to Calcutta, once said:

> God speaks in the silence of the heart,
> and we listen.

We have to be still, be silent, to hear God. When our stillness before God vanishes, so does the peace within our souls; this is when doubt can begin to set in.

Jesus is also telling us the same thing in Mark. Jesus tells the Parable of the Sower and then later explains it to His disciples. For this particular verse, I like The Message translation:

> "The seed cast in the weeds represents the ones who hear the kingdom news but are overwhelmed with worries about all the things they have to do and all the things they want to get. The stress strangles what they heard, and nothing comes of it"
> (Mark 4:18-19, The Message).

The word "worries" from verse 19 is translated from the Greek word *merimna*, which means:

> Separated from the whole; (figuratively) worry (anxiety), dividing and fracturing a person's being into parts.

In this passage, *merimna* refers to anxiety about things pertaining to this earthly life. Wow, we hear God's word, but life takes over and drowns out God and His word. There have been countless occasions where I've found myself running around nonstop, taking care of the various tasks that come with daily life. At the end of the day, and sometimes even after a few days, I realize I haven't spoken to God. It grieves my soul. All the while, the demons are rejoicing.

Busyness can many times be due to worry. Jesus, as He spoke to His followers, tells us in Matthew 6:25-34 not to worry about everyday life and to seek the kingdom of God. It's essential to understand that concern and worry are not the same thing. Concern acknowledges that something needs to be done: seek God and move into action. Worry is giving into consuming fear and agitation, leaving God out of the picture. Another way to view the difference between concern and worry: You are in control of concern; worry is in control of you.

The story in Luke, where Jesus goes to Mary and Martha's house, tells us what Jesus says about being too busy, too busy for Him.

> Now as they were traveling along, He entered a village; and a woman named Martha welcomed Him into her home. And she had a sister called Mary, who was also seated at the Lord's feet, and was listening to His word. But Martha was distracted with all her preparations; and she came up to Him and said, "Lord, do You not care that my sister has left me to do the serving by myself? Then tell her to help me." But the Lord answered and said to her, "Martha, Martha, you are worried and distracted by many things; but only one thing is necessary;

for Mary has chosen the good part, which shall
not be taken away from her"
(Luke 10:38-42, NASB).

Here are a few interesting points about this passage of Scripture. In verse 40, the word "distracted" is translated from the Greek word *perispaó*. This passage is the only place in Scripture where this word is used. It means:

> To draw away, distract; to be driven about
> mentally, to be distracted: to be over-occupied,
> too busy, about a thing.

Are you ever *perispaó*? I know I am. Martha was distracted, too busy, drawn away. On the other hand, Mary sat close to Jesus, at His feet, to listen to what He had to say. Here, the word "listen" is translated from the Greek word *akouó*, which means:

> To listen, hear, comprehend.

Mary listened, heard, and comprehended what Jesus said. Frustrated, Martha asked Jesus, "'Do You not care that my sister [isn't helping me]?'" Jesus' response began with "'Martha, Martha.'" Did Jesus answer Martha in anger to her question, her accusation? No, not at all. In biblical times, one repeated a name twice prior to saying something important or expressing a close relationship with that person; it was an intimate expression.[c]

There are only eight times in the Bible where God (Jesus) calls someone by name twice:

> Abraham (Genesis 22:11)
> Jacob (Genesis 46:2)
> Moses (Exodus 3:4)
> Samuel (1 Samuel 3:10)
> Martha (Luke 10:41)
> Simon (Luke 22:31)
> My God (Jesus quoting Psalm 22:1 in
>   Matthew 27:46 and Mark 15:34)
> Saul (Acts 9:4)

Having an intimate relationship with Jesus and hearing Him call your name twice would be amazing. Maybe one day I will hear Him say, "Tracy, Tracy, you finished the race well."

Jesus told Martha she had it wrong; Mary had it right. Jesus pointed out that she was distracted and worried about many things. Martha had Jesus in her house, and she wasn't paying attention to Him because she was distracted with, most likely, preparing a meal and being a good hostess. Hospitality was a big deal in biblical times. Jesus said to Martha, "'But only one thing is necessary.'" Jesus told Martha that all her running around was unnecessary and that the only thing necessary was Him. Then Jesus said, "'Mary has chosen the good part which shall not be taken away from her.'" Mary had it right; she spent time with Jesus, listened to Him, learned from Him, and grew her relationship with Him.

Do you see yourself in any of these barriers? If we are honest, we probably experience all four barriers at some point in our lives. Recognize these barriers in your life, and always thank God for all the blessings He has bestowed upon you. As you build a close relationship with God, the barriers will fade.

———————◆●◆———————

Thankfulness flows out of our relationship with God. Make a conscious effort to see your many blessings, focus on what God graciously gives you, and thank Him daily. We need to be mindful of distractions that can take our focus away from God, such as materialism, comparison, pride, and busyness. Never let concerns become worry; worry is all-consuming. In this world, it's easy to spiral away from God; we must be diligent in our daily walk with Him.

It is impossible for
gratitude and discontent to exist
in the same heart

CHAPTER 5

Comparison

Comparing ourselves to others harms the soul and pulls us away from our relationship with God. Each of us has a unique purpose and plan that God has designed for us, and it's important to focus on fulfilling that plan rather than worrying about what God has planned for others. As we continue to follow God and strengthen our relationship with Him, He entrusts us with more here on Earth. By being faithful with our blessings in this world, we store up treasures in Heaven. However, it's difficult to store up treasures if our focus is on others and not on what we are entrusted with. We need to look at God's provision in our lives. God knows what we need, and He provides. Comparison is an attitude of dissatisfaction with God's provision for one's life that leads to an obsession with having more.[a] This chapter will look at ways to avoid the pit of comparison.

What does the wisest man of the Old Testament have to say about comparison? Solomon writes in Ecclesiastes:

And I saw that all toil and all achievement spring from one person's envy of another. This too is meaningless, a chasing after the wind (Ecclesiastes 4:4, NIV).

It's meaningless. The word "meaningless" is translated from the Hebrew word *hebel*, which means:

Delusion, emptiness, futile, futility, useless, worthless.

Comparison is dangerous to the soul. Yet, it can be so hard to avoid. A saying I grew up with was, "Keeping up with the Joneses." This phrase referred to the tendency to desire what our neighbors have and even strive to acquire something better. This mindset can lead us into trouble in more ways than one. Comparison quickly steals our joy, leaving us frustrated, bitter, and ungrateful towards God. The crazy thing is we can feel this way and not even realize it's due to comparison!

In a spiritual sense, comparison leads to discontentment, leading to ingratitude. Comparison leads to a desire for more, which can lead to sin and rebellion against God. If we are consumed by what others have and what we don't have, it can lead us to go to any length to get what we want. This can cause us to lose sight of God, engage in unethical behavior, and even lead us down a path of self-destruction. Comparison leads us to turn inward, focus on ourselves, and be self-centered.

What is the antidote to comparison? Contentment and a grateful heart. Being content is being at peace with the unchangeable circumstances, choices, and mistakes that shape our future. We need to be satisfied with what God so graciously gives us. Instead of looking inward, look outward for things you can do to help others. Taking the focus off self and helping others does incredible things for the soul.

God Has a Plan for Us

God has a purpose and plan for each of us. As Paul explains,

> For we are His workmanship, created in Christ Jesus for good works, which God prepared beforehand so that we would walk in them (Ephesians 2:10, NASB).

The word "workmanship" is translated from the Greek word *poiéma*, which gives us our English words "poem" and "poetry." This Greek word appears only twice in the New Testament (Ephesians 2:10, Romans 1:20). *Poiéma* means "what has been made." God created us; we are His poem, His work of art, His masterpiece. When we accept Jesus as our savior, we are "created in Christ Jesus." We are spiritually transformed, reborn, and ready to be used by God. The passage states, "which God prepared beforehand." He set our paths before we were created.

God's plan for your life is unique. Whatever God entrusts you with, be a good steward, and don't worry about what God has entrusted to others. God gives us what we can handle, and He gives to us to grow us. It's up to us to follow Him. Strive to follow what God has set before you—His plan for your life.

Little and Much

What God gives us is based upon what we do with what He has already given. It has nothing to do with anyone else; it's only between us and God. The more we are given, the greater the expectation.

> "But someone who does not know, and then does something wrong, will be punished only lightly. When someone has been given much, much will be required in return; and when someone has been entrusted with much, even more will be required" (Luke 12:48, NLT).

In Luke 12, Jesus teaches His disciples that if someone is entrusted with much, much is required in return. Although this passage refers to the judgment, we can apply this principle to every aspect of our lives. Everything we have—our lives, our families, our health, our mental capacity, our abilities, our jobs, and our homes—is given to us by the graciousness of God.

Don't misunderstand this principle by assuming that those with less have less responsibility; that isn't true. Whether we are entrusted with little or much, our ultimate responsibility remains the same—to use the things given to us to glorify God and to help others. The only difference is how much we are responsible for.

Luke 12 ties into a passage in Matthew 25 where Jesus tells the Parable of the Three Servants. This parable deals with the kingdom of Heaven and the Master leaving and coming back and seeing what His servants have done with what He entrusted to them. Although I'm not going into the details of the parable, there is a portion of it that I want to focus on:

> "To one he gave five talents, to another, two, and to another, one, each according to his own ability; and he went on his journey" (Matthew 25:15, NASB).

The Master (Jesus) gave according to each person's ability. The Master knew the servants and how much responsibility He could entrust to each. Each servant had the opportunity to "grow" what they were given while the Master was away. God has a plan for each of us, and He gives to us according to our abilities. Many times, God will give us something that causes us to strive and also stumble and fall along the way. What He gives may not be in our current reach, but the ability to reach resides within us; this is one of the ways God grows us.

Then, the Master came back from his journey.

> "His master said to him, 'Well done, good and faithful servant. You have been faithful and trustworthy over a little, I will put you in charge of many things; share in the joy of your master'" (Matthew 25:21, 23, AMP).

The Master (Jesus) said this to both the servant with the five talents and the servant with the two talents. Jesus didn't expect both servants to produce the same but for each one to produce proportionally to the abilities they had. Because the servants were faithful with what they were given, the Master put them in charge of many things. In this parable, the Master went on a journey that correlates to Jesus' ascension from Earth into Heaven. The Master returned from his journey, which correlates to the return of Christ and His judgment of both believers and unbelievers. As Christians, our faithfulness in this world will determine our rewards in the next.

Matthew 25 and another passage in Luke 16 demonstrate the relationship between little and much.[b] Matthew 25 addresses how we serve God; Luke 16 addresses how we use our wealth.

> "If you are faithful in little things, you will be
> faithful in large ones. But if you are dishonest in
> little things, you won't be honest with greater
> responsibilities. And if you are untrustworthy
> about worldly wealth, who will trust you with
> the true riches of heaven? And if you are not
> faithful with other people's things, why should
> you be trusted with things of your own?"
> (Luke 16:10-12, NLT).

This passage is deep, and we are going to break it down. Jesus uses the words "wealth" and "riches," which we discussed in Chapter 4. When Jesus speaks of "worldly wealth," He is talking about this world; when He is speaking of "true riches," He is talking about the spiritual blessings we will receive in the world to come. Jesus is talking about little and much; there is a relationship between the two. What we do with little is a clear indication of what we will do with much. You can view this statement in both a positive and a negative way.

Jesus is observing how we use the wealth we possess in this present world. The things of this world are not our own;

they are temporal. In this parable, "other people's things" can be viewed in two ways. Firstly, from a worldly perspective, someone on Earth entrusts you with something. Secondly, from a godly perspective, meaning God entrusts you with something. God gives us what we have here on Earth, either directly or through others, and we are to be good stewards of what we are entrusted with.

The "little" concerns what we do or don't do in this world with what we are given; the "much" concerns the spiritual blessings we will be given in our eternal dwelling place.

This truth, through our worldly lens, seems backward. We typically think of someone caring for their things better than someone else's. Here, God is saying if you cannot be faithful with another's things, He will not entrust you with more in this world, nor will He give you things of your own in eternity. Jesus tells us in Revelation:

> "Behold, I (Jesus) am coming quickly, and My reward is with Me, to give to each one according to the merit of his deeds (earthly works, faithfulness)"
> (Revelation 22:12, AMP).

We receive rewards in Heaven based on what we do here on Earth. We won't be equal in Heaven; we will have rewards, jobs, and responsibilities based on how we handled what we were entrusted with on Earth. Things given to us in Heaven will never be taken away or lost.

Take what God gives you—your talents, opportunities, relationships, and blessings—and strive to be faithful with them. Then, one day, your rewards will be bountiful in eternity.

The parable in Luke 16 also applies to our daily lives as we interact with others. If we demonstrate that we can do the small things well, we will be given bigger things to achieve. For instance, if we perform well at work, we are given more tasks and responsibilities. Similarly, if children show responsibility with small privileges, they earn more privileges. On the negative side, if we cannot do the small things well, we are not trusted to do larger things. Why is that? The small things make up the larger things. It's in the small things that we demonstrate our abilities, work ethic, and our trustworthiness to handle the big things.

God's Provision

God's provision in your life comes from His goodness; therefore, be grateful for what He has already provided. God knows what you need, and it's often not what you think you need. Many times, we confuse what we want with what we need. God sees what we need even when we cannot. This is God's providential care—He loves and cares for us. From a worldly perspective, some seem to have more than others. As we look around, there will always be someone who has the bigger house, drives the fancier car, and earns more money; just because someone appears to have more on the outside certainly does not mean they have more on the inside. What matters is what is in the heart. Are you constantly comparing yourself to others, or are you content and thankful for what you have? A person can have an abundant bank account but be spiritually bankrupt. A fancier car does not mean you know where you are going. A bigger house does not make a home. It's better to have a home full of love than a mansion without it. God is concerned with what we do with what we're given; we need to focus on what we're given and be faithful in that rather than wonder why we were not given more. Be grateful for what God entrusts you with; God knows what is best for you.

God gives us free will. We choose how we are going to live our lives each day. Are we going to live a life of discontentment or a life of gratitude? It's impossible for gratitude and discontent to exist in the same heart. The truly successful person is the one who knows the will of God and does it. This person will receive blessings beyond measure. The received blessing may not always be in this life but certainly will be in the next.

I once heard a pastor say, "If you do not pursue your calling, you will spend your entire life wishing you were someone else." There is a lot of wisdom in that statement.

Avoid the Pit

So, how can we avoid the pit of comparison?[c]

1. Focus on God

When we focus on ourselves in comparison to others, we see our perceived shortcomings. When we look inward, we tend to believe others are stronger or more intelligent than we are or that they have more opportunities—in essence, we assume they have a better life. What are we doing? We are taking our eyes off God. The exodus from Egypt gives us a great example of the Israelites taking their eyes off God and looking inward.

In Numbers 13, God ordered Moses to send twelve spies into the Promised Land. The Israelites had already experienced God's deliverance from Egypt firsthand. God told them that He was going to give them the Promised Land. But what did ten of them do? They took their eyes off God, the God who had already performed so many miracles before their eyes, the God who told them He would deliver them into the Promised Land. They became overwhelmed by the giants in the land. The Anakites who resided in the Promised Land were an intimidating race of giant, warlike people (Numbers 13:28-33). The ten spies saw people who were physically bigger and stronger and never even thought about what God had promised them. They focused inward:

> "We even saw giants there, the descendants of
> Anak. Next to them, we felt like grasshoppers,
> and that's what they thought, too!"
> (Numbers 13:33, NLT).

But what about the other two spies, Caleb and Joshua? They stayed focused on God:

> But Caleb tried to quiet the people as they
> stood before Moses. "Let's go at once to take
> the land," he said. "We can certainly conquer it!"
> (Numbers 13:30, NLT).

When all was said and done, God punished the Israelites for their rebellion and for not trusting Him; He sentenced them to wander in the desert for forty years. No male over twenty who rebelled against God would enter the Promised Land. Among the spies, only Caleb and Joshua would enter.

> "You will not enter and occupy the land I swore to give you. The only exceptions will be Caleb son of Jephunneh and Joshua son of Nun" (Numbers 14:30, NLT).

2. Avoid an Attitude of Entitlement

We can fall into the pit of comparison due to a sense of entitlement. It's easy to feel that we deserve the same opportunities as others. When we don't receive what we want, or others receive what we think they don't deserve, we tend to think things are unfair. If we feel entitled, our relationship with God will be diminished. Why is that? Essentially, we get angry with God, and we pull away from him. When we feel entitled, we value ourselves above all relationships, including our relationship with our Heavenly Father.

Although the Bible does not explicitly use the word entitled, it definitely speaks to the attitude. Jesus tells the Parable of the Lost Son (Luke 15:11-32), which demonstrates this attitude. The younger son demanded his inheritance from his father. This displays an attitude of entitlement because, by custom, the inheritance wasn't given until the father died. The father gave the inheritance to the younger son, and he went off and squandered it. He then humbly came back to his father. The father celebrated because he had his son return home. The older son became angry and told his father, "but he replied, 'All these years I've slaved for you and never once refused to do a single thing you told me to. And in all that time you never gave me even one young goat for a feast with my friends. Yet when this son of yours comes back after squandering your money on prostitutes, you celebrate by killing the fattened calf!'" (Luke 15:29-30, NLT).

The older son's attitude is also a form of entitlement. He felt the younger son didn't deserve a celebratory feast. He felt slighted.

When we are in need and receive a blessing that fulfills that need, we should be grateful rather than complaining about why we didn't receive more blessings. Similarly, we should rejoice with others rather than feel jealous or resentful when they receive a blessing.

Entitlement is concerned with demanding our rights with God and then resenting others who are the object of our envy. We need to get past the sin of entitlement and recognize that what we have is because of God's grace. Once we do this, we will be able to see things from a different perspective.

3. Be Grateful for All God's Blessings

When we stop and take inventory of how God blesses us and see God's grace in our lives, it allows us to see even the smallest of blessings and, in turn, become more thankful and gracious. We need to thank God for all our blessings, no matter how big or small. We are not only to show our gratitude to God for our blessings; we need to share what God has done for us with others. Focus your eyes on God, reflect, and remember how He has worked in your life and the blessings He has given.

4. Rejoice With Others

Be grateful to God for how He works in other people's lives. Their success isn't a reflection of you; someone else's success does not mean you're a failure. We need to eliminate that kind of thinking. It also does not mean that God loves them more than us. Paul tells us to rejoice with those who rejoice and weep with those who weep (Romans 12:15).

Rejoice; be happy for those who are happy. Be thankful when we see the blessings in others' lives. It's exciting to see God working in others, bringing them blessings and miracles. When we see God move in others' lives, remember that we are seeing God move, and we need to rejoice. Be thankful for God's blessings, even when those blessings fall directly upon others. After all, we serve a God who generously blesses all who belong to Him.

5. See Others' Needs

When we choose to fix our eyes on God, that, in turn, helps us to see others as God sees them. We can then be outward-looking, not comparing ourselves to others but seeing how we can bless others and meet their needs. Look around; we can be a blessing to others in many ways. Something as simple as a smile, a friendly greeting, an encouraging word, or physically opening a door for someone can brighten their day. We need to be willing to listen to someone share what is on their heart, really listen to them, and not turn the conversation to ourselves.

These are a few things we can do in the ordinary course of our days. For instance, we can lend a hand to our neighbors with their yard work or offer to watch their kids while they run errands. You could help someone with their homework or study for an exam. Preparing meals when someone has a sick family member or quietly sitting with someone who is broken are other ways to be a blessing. Volunteering at a homeless shelter or your local food bank is also an excellent opportunity to make a difference in someone's life. Can I let you in on a secret? When we reach out and bless others, guess what? The blessing comes back to us tenfold. It's such a blessing to bless others. Solomon tells us, "He who waters will himself be watered [reaping the generosity he has sown]" (Proverbs 11:25, AMP). There is much wisdom in this verse; blessing others does so much for the soul.

6. Don't Let Desires Turn into Idols

What is an idol? We tend to think about biblical times when people worshiped false gods and carved images of their false gods. These carved images were idols. Since we don't bow down to a carved statue, we think we don't worship idols. However, an idol is anything that is more important to us than God. Anything that consumes our thoughts, wants, and desires more than God. An idol might include our job, spouse, children, friends, technology, power, notoriety, money, or material possessions. We become idolatrous when we desire the created more than the Creator. Idolatry looks different today than it did in biblical times, but unfortunately, it's still very prevalent today. Essentially, an idol is anything that takes the place of God as our most important focus and priority.

The Bible speaks about idolatry in both the Old and New Testaments, and none of it's good. John gets right to the point when he tells us to keep ourselves from idols (1 John 5:21).

7. Find Your Identity in Christ

We tend to look at others from the outside—what job they have, where they live, what kind of car they drive, what position they have at work or in society. We also tend to look at ourselves and value ourselves in terms of what society tells us. What is our job, how much money do we earn, what is our standing in society, does everyone know us, are we the most beautiful, are we the stars of the game? Why do we try to stand out in the ever-changing view of society? Great today, not so great tomorrow. It's impossible to know who we are when we place our identity in something that continually changes.

We are not to find our identity in this world; we are to find our identity in Jesus Christ. What does that mean? We are who God says we are, not who others say or think we are. God says you are His; you are fearfully and wonderfully made. Don't try to please man; strive to please God. Unlike this world, God is the same yesterday, today, and tomorrow; He does not change. In the book of Colossians, Paul tells us:

> Work willingly at whatever you do, as though you were working for the Lord rather than for people. Remember that the Lord will give you an inheritance as your reward, and that the Master you are serving is Christ (Colossians 3:23-24, NLT).

Remember not who you are but *whose* you are.

Comparison takes our eyes off God and brings us down emotionally. It's easy to find someone who appears to have more, but instead, focus on your blessings. God is sovereign; He controls all. He knows our needs, and He provides. Remember, everything we have on the face of this Earth is freely given to us by God, including our family, health, opportunities, jobs, and, yes, even material possessions. We are merely stewards of what we are given. All our possessions will be left behind when we pass from this Earth. What we possess on Earth is only temporary, and it isn't truly ours. God watches how we care for what we are entrusted with on Earth. If we are faithful with what we are given, He will give us more to take care of. How we take care of things we are entrusted with here on Earth will determine what we will be given, our rewards, in Heaven. We can be good stewards by focusing on what we are blessed with and passing those blessings on to others. Avoid the pit of comparison; it pulls our focus away from God. Rejoice with others as God blesses them. Always keep God first, and never let anything become an idol in your life. Remember to find your identity in Jesus Christ; we are who God says we are, not what others say or think we are. Always remain in God's word.

A final note on comparison: It isn't a sin to want more and to work for more as long as God remains the priority and we don't lose sight of Him.

Our outward circumstances
don't have to dictate
our outward response

CHAPTER 6

God Hates Grumbling

We have discussed gratitude, but have you ever considered its opposite? The Bible calls it "grumbling," which means complaining and showing ingratitude. Sometimes, we try to gloss over our grumbling by saying things such as, "I just needed to vent" or "I need to get this off my chest." Maybe we can fool other people, but we can never fool God. When we outwardly complain to others about our life's circumstances, we display our ingratitude towards God, and, in the process, we rob others of their joy. Let's look at what grumbling does to us and those around us.

Grumbling Affects Those Around Us

Grumbling has the potential to bring people down and create a barrier between them and God. In the Garden of Eden, Satan spoke negatively about God to Eve (Genesis 3:4), which led to Adam and Eve eating from the tree of the knowledge of good and evil. This drove a wedge between man and God, creating a barrier that separated them.

In the Garden of Eden, God told Adam that he could freely eat of any tree in the garden, just not from the tree of the knowledge of good and evil. Although we don't know how many trees were in the Garden, Scripture tells us, "God made all sorts of trees" (Genesis 2:9, NLT). The tree of the knowledge of good and evil was placed in the middle of the garden. This tree wasn't tucked away, out of sight. Adam and Eve continually saw this tree as they went about their day. God abundantly provided food for Adam and Eve. Then, Satan appeared, the embodiment of negativity, and drew Eve's attention to the forbidden tree. Satan took Eve's focus from all the good that she had around her and brought it to the one thing she could not have. Complaining does something similar. When we complain to others, we take their mind off the goodness and can cause them to focus, even momentarily, on the negative.

So, did Eve look at all the trees she could freely eat from? No, with the prompting of Satan, she focused on the one she wasn't to eat from. She focused on the negative, not the good. Focusing on what she could not have caused discontentment. Pointing out the negative can take the focus off the positive.

Years ago, I shared an office with a co-worker who had a very negative attitude. Every time she spoke, it was negative. There was constant negativity spewing at me all day long. After a while, it wore me down; I was exhausted. Negativity brings unrest and makes the soul weary. No one likes to be around a person who is constantly grumbling. Proverbs contains much wisdom and has numerous verses concerning the tongue, a most powerful muscle.

The tongue can bring death or life;
  those who love to talk will reap
  the consequences (Proverbs 18:21, NLT).

This co-worker's tongue spoke death and was a drain on everyone around her. She did reap the consequences; she lived a miserable life of complaining and never appeared to have joy or happiness.

Grumbling Shows Ingratitude

Grumbling to others shows ingratitude towards God. When we have an ungrateful heart, it shows up in our speech.

No one gives us more than God; He gives us our physical, spiritual, and eternal life and sustains us on Earth. God wants us to recognize all He does and show gratitude.

As a parent, imagine taking your child out for a fun-filled day. You take them to play putt-putt golf, eat at their favorite fast-food restaurant, and buy them a trendy new T-shirt. However, on your way back home, your child insists on stopping for ice cream. You explain to them that it's getting late, and you need to get back home to prepare dinner and get ready for the next day. Unfortunately, your child gets angry and remains upset throughout the evening. As a parent, it can be disheartening to spend several hours doing things for and with your child and then to be met with anger when you deny their request. It can leave you feeling unappreciated and hurt. Now, think about how God feels when we get "mad" because we don't get what we want or things don't go our way.

Not getting what they wanted according to their timetable was the case with the Israelites; they were complainers and ungrateful. During their exodus from Egypt, the Israelites complained as they arrived at the Red Sea with the pursuing Egyptians behind them:

> As Pharaoh approached, the people of Israel looked up and panicked when they saw the Egyptians overtaking them. They cried out to the LORD, and they said to Moses, "Why did you bring us out here to die in the wilderness? Weren't there enough graves for us in Egypt? What have you done to us? Why did you make us leave Egypt? Didn't we tell you this would happen while we were still in Egypt? We said, 'Leave us alone! Let us be slaves to the Egyptians. It's better to be a slave in Egypt than a corpse in the wilderness!'"
> (Exodus 14:10-12, NIV).

God delivered them. After crossing the Red Sea, the people sang a song of deliverance unto God (Exodus 15:1-18). After three days, they arrived at the oasis of Marah, where the water was bitter and undrinkable. As expected, the Israelites complained once again.

> So the people grumbled against Moses, saying, "What are we to drink?" (Exodus 15:24, NIV).

God gave them water. God instructed Moses to throw a piece of wood into the water, and the water was then good to drink.

After leaving Marah, they reached the oasis of Elim and then continued their journey into the wilderness, the Desert of Sin.

> In the desert the whole community grumbled against Moses and Aaron. The Israelites said to them, "If only we had died by the LORD's hand in Egypt! There we sat around pots of meat and ate all the food we wanted, but you have brought us out into this desert to starve this entire assembly to death"
> (Exodus 16:2-3, NIV).

> Moses also said, "You will know that it was the LORD when he gives you meat to eat in the evening and all the bread you want in the morning because he has heard your grumbling against him. Who are we? You are not grumbling against us but against the LORD"
> (Exodus 16:8, NIV).

God provided. From the Desert of Sin, they traveled and camped at Rephidim. Once again, they grumbled.

> But the people were thirsty for water there, and they grumbled against Moses. They said, "Why did you bring us up out of Egypt to make us and our children and livestock die of thirst?" (Exodus 17:3, NIV).

Again, God provided.

Many times, the object of our desires isn't wrong. In the passages above, the Israelites wanted food, water, and safety provisions. Their need was genuine, but they wanted these good things more than God Himself. The problem was they never *asked* God for these things. Instead, they complained and grumbled to God and Moses. If they had asked God and not grumbled against Him, God may have answered their need sooner. In the New Testament, James tells us that we do not have because we do not ask God (James 4:2).

Grumbling Causes Forgetfulness

The Israelites didn't remember how God had repeatedly provided for them. He had brought them out of Egypt, and they witnessed miracle after miracle. God always supplied their needs.

Psalms even speaks of the Israelites forgetting all God had done for them:

> Yet how quickly they forgot what he had done!
>   They wouldn't wait for his counsel!
> In the wilderness their desires ran wild,
>   testing God's patience in that dry wasteland
> (Psalm 106:13-14, NLT).

The Israelites' desires ran wild. We need to be careful as well. We need to ensure that our desires don't run wild and become expectations and that our expectations don't turn into a sense of entitlement.

Do Not Grumble

What does Paul tell us about grumbling in the New Testament? Paul tells us in Philippians:

> Do everything without grumbling or arguing, so that you may be blameless and pure, children of God without blemish though you live in a crooked and perverse society, in which you shine as lights in the world
> (Philippians 2:14-15, NET).

Did I read that right? Do *everything* without grumbling. I prefer to do "most" things without grumbling. Oh, how easy it is to grumble and complain and not even realize we are doing it. Refraining from grumbling is hard. Grumbling is a sin that we don't tend to think about. We tend to overlook it in others and certainly don't consider our valid complaints as being sinful. However, God's word tells us otherwise.

Back to Philippians 2:15, the words "without blemish" are translated from the Greek word *amomos*, which means:

> Faultless, unblameable, (figuratively) morally, spiritually blameless, unblemished from the marring effects of sin.

Paul, in Philippians 2:14-15, says that the children of God are not to be fault-finders and complainers. We are to be morally and spiritually blameless so that we will shine as a light in this crooked and perverse world.

When Paul wrote Philippians, he was in prison, in shackles. What can we learn from that? Our outward circumstances don't have to dictate our outward response.

Rely on God

When we grumble, it comes from within. Grumbling does not start with an outward expression. It begins within our hearts and makes its way out through our attitude and our speech. Therefore, it's essential to let the Holy Spirit dictate our response and rely on God's grace, not the world that Satan rules. When we grumble, we give Satan a foothold and open ourselves up to his lies. We live in this world, but we don't have to be of this world; I know this is hard. We need to draw close to our Heavenly Father and ask Him for His strength and help.

> Hold firmly to the word of life; then, on the day of Christ's return, I will be proud that I did not run the race in vain and that my work was not useless (Philippians 2:16, NLT).

The "word of life" is the gospel, the good news of Jesus Christ. When Paul wrote, "Hold firmly to the word of life," he was saying to know Jesus in your heart and hold firmly to His teachings. What is Paul saying when he says he did not run the race in vain? The Christian life is a race. The word "vain" is translated from the Greek word *kenos*, which means:

Empty, worthless.

We are not to race against an empty life, a wasted life. We need to follow Jesus and let others see Him in us. We need to spread

Jesus' truth and love. Is it hard to follow Christ in this world? Absolutely. That is why we run and labor in His name. At the coming of Christ, we will know, without a doubt, that we didn't run life's race in vain. When we meet those in Heaven whom we impacted while on Earth, we will see that our efforts were not in vain. Was it worth all the hard work and effort? Absolutely! We ran and labored for the glory of Christ.

Expressing Our Dissatisfaction

How do we express the dissatisfaction we experience to God? Does all this mean we cannot complain to God? So, let's step back and parse the words here. Understanding the difference between complaining *to* God and grumbling *against* God is vital. There are two ways to show our dissatisfaction or hurt, the first being grumbling. Grumbling is inwardly complaining to ourselves or outwardly complaining to others and, in essence, showing no faith in God; it's complaining with an impure heart. It's essentially accusing God of not doing the right thing. This type of complaining—grumbling—is sinful. One of the consequences of grumbling is that we arouse God's anger. Numbers tells us that God is displeased with the grumbling Israelites; they have provoked Him repeatedly, and now He burns with anger.

> Now when the people complained, it displeased the LORD; for the LORD heard it, and His anger was aroused. So the fire of the LORD burned among them, and consumed some in the outskirts of the camp (Numbers 11:1, NKJV).

God warned them by sending a fire that burned part of their camp. Yet, they still didn't get it.

> The LORD said to Moses and Aaron: "How long will this wicked community grumble against me? I have heard the complaints of these grumbling Israelites"
> (Numbers 14:26-27, NIV).

We can sense the exasperation in God's voice.

Then, there is complaining with a pure heart directly to God. A complaining that does not accuse or imply that God has done something wrong or has done nothing at all. Complaining with a pure heart is pure, honest, raw emotion, crying out to God about the hurt, disappointment, and anxiety of living in this broken world that Satan temporarily rules. This is demonstrated in Psalms as David pours out his heart to God while in the cave of Adullam:

> I cry aloud to the LORD;
>   I lift up my voice to the LORD for mercy.
> I pour out before him my complaint;
>   before him I tell my trouble
> (Psalm 142:1-2, NIV).

In the New Testament, Peter and Paul tell us:

> Cast all your anxiety on him because he cares for you (1 Peter 5:7, NIV).

> Do not be anxious about anything,
> but in everything, by prayer and petition,

with thanksgiving, present your requests
to God (Philippians 4:6, NIV).

We need to take our disappointments and frustrations to our Heavenly Father. Let His words and promises remind us of His goodness and unfailing love. Otherwise, our desires can quickly turn into discontentment and grumbling.

Does that mean we should not talk to friends or family about our feelings? Of course, we should, but we need to speak with a pure heart, not a heart of anger and discontent. It's not always what we say but our attitude when we say it.

Avoid Grumbling

What can we do to avoid grumbling?

1. Pray

Pray and express our dissatisfaction, hurts, wants, and desires directly to God. He already knows them; talk to Him about it. Ask Him for help to change your attitude toward the situation.

2. Remember

It's essential for us to remember all the good things God has done for us in the past and how He is always faithful. One effective way to do this is by keeping a prayer journal. Write down and date prayer requests. When you receive an answer, write and date that next to the request. Doing this helps us to remember. We can go back and read how God has answered our prayers. When we are in the midst of a trial, a need, or a frustration, it's easy to forget what He has done for us in the past.

3. Be Content

Be content with the blessings God has provided. Paul tells us that he learned to be content in every circumstance (Philippians 4:11). Paul is the epitome of contentment; he endured much persecution during his ministry. Paul then tells us that godliness with contentment is great gain (1 Timothy 6:6). When we live in a way that is pleasing and honoring to God and are content with what we possess, we most likely have a strong spiritual life. We need a strong spiritual life to help us navigate life's difficulties and challenges and remain content in the process. Navigating life's challenges in a manner that is pleasing to God is great gain.

4. Be Grateful

Express gratitude to God for all He has done, including what He is currently doing behind the scenes that you are unaware of. Be grateful for all that you have, even in difficult times. When we express our gratitude to God, we strengthen our relationship with Him.

———————●●————————

It's important to remember that grumbling can negatively impact someone's day and put a wedge between them and God. As Christians, it's essential to be mindful of our words and how they reflect upon our faith. Grumbling isn't a good witness for Christ. Instead, express your heart to God and ask Him to help you through your discouragement and discontent. Rely on Him to guide you through your current circumstances and communicate with your loved ones with a pure heart. Chapter 9 will offer valuable insights into maintaining a positive outlook, which can help you avoid grumbling.

Pride is a heart issue

CHAPTER 7

Beware of Pride

P ride is one of the most destructive sins; it destroys us from within by pulling us away from God. Proverbs tell us a couple of things about pride. Firstly, it tells us that God hates pride (Proverbs 8:13), and secondly, pride leads to disgrace (Proverbs 11:2). Proverbs 6 lists things that the Lord hates; the first is pride:

> These six things the LORD hates,
> Yes, seven, are an abomination to Him:
> A proud look,
> A lying tongue,
> Hands that shed innocent blood,
> A heart that devises wicked plans,
> Feet that are swift in running to evil,
> A false witness who speaks lies,
> And one who sows discord among brethren
> (Proverbs 6:16-19, NKJV).

A worldly definition of pride is:[a]

> A feeling of deep pleasure or satisfaction derived
> from one's own achievements, the achievements
> of those with whom one is closely associated,
> or from qualities or possessions that are widely
> admired.

The Devil's Sin

Pride is the devil's sin. Pride was the first sin committed in the universe, in God's creation. Satan, known as Lucifer before his fall (Isaiah 14:12, KJV), was the chief angel. There are two passages in the Old Testament that many theologians believe talk about the fall of Satan: Isaiah 14 and Ezekiel 28.[b] We will look at Ezekiel, where we find Ezekiel prophesying against the prince and the king of Tyre. In the first ten verses of chapter 28, Ezekiel prophesies against the prince of Tyre, the city's leader. His fundamental sin was pride.

In Ezekiel 28:12, God tells Ezekiel to take up a lament concerning the king of Tyre. So, who is the king? The king is the ruler over the prince, the spiritual ruler. In Ezekiel, God talks about the physical ruler—the prince—and the spiritual ruler—Satan. Ezekiel goes on to describe Satan's perfection:

> The word of the LORD came to me: "Son of man,
> take up a lament concerning the king of Tyre and
> say to him: 'This is what the Sovereign LORD says:
> "'You were the seal of perfection,
> full of wisdom and perfect in beauty'"
> (Ezekiel 28:11-12, NIV).

In God's words, Satan was the "seal of perfection." In biblical times, a seal represented a token of authenticity, effectively saying Satan was authentically perfect. Then, God describes Satan's pride:

> "'Your heart became proud
>   on account of your beauty,
> and you corrupted your wisdom
>   because of your splendor.
> So I threw you to the earth;
>   I made a spectacle of you before kings'"
> (Ezekiel 28:17, NIV).

Most of the time, proud people tend to be proud of something that isn't true. They think too highly of themselves, which is self-deception. In the case of Satan's pride, he was indeed the most beautiful. Even though what he was proud of was true, what did God do to him? God threw Satan down to Earth, the ground, and made a spectacle of him. God created Satan; everything Satan had was freely given to him by God. We need to remember that God created us, and everything we have is freely given to us by God. Pride discounts God.

In Matthew, Jesus tells us:

> "'You must love the LORD your God with all
> your heart, all your soul, and all your mind.'
> This is the first and greatest commandment"
> (Matthew 22:37-38, NLT).

We can understand why God hates pride. Pride is putting ourselves above God, breaking the first and greatest commandment. Jesus' commandment in Matthew leaves no room for selfish pride.

Downfalls of Pride

Satan's number one goal is to set creation against God. Satan wants us to think that life apart from God is possible and preferable. It takes pride and arrogance to believe that we don't need God and that our will should be above God's will. In reality, what does pride do to us? What did it do to Satan? It leads to ingratitude. If we are proud, it's all about us, what we did, and who we think we are. There is no room for thankfulness when a heart is full of pride. We don't believe we need to be thankful because, in our minds, we accomplished everything on our own. Once we become ungracious, we then become independent from God. We think we don't need God; we can do everything ourselves. Then, of course, this leads to a lack of relationship with God. In Chapter 2, we saw how vital a relationship with our Heavenly Father is.

Pride causes us to compete and compare, forgetting to love those around us. The proud are lovers of self. Everything is about them, their wants, their wishes. At the root of pride is the desire for power. Not only do the proud want to control their destiny, but they also want to control the destiny of others. The proud man believes he is the master of his fate but fails to understand that pride goes before a fall. As Proverbs instructs,

> Pride goes before destruction,
> and haughtiness before a fall
> (Proverbs 16:18, NLT).

Likewise,

> Haughtiness goes before destruction;
>   humility precedes honor
> (Proverbs 18:12, NLT).

The word "haughtiness" is a synonym for arrogance. Remember, arrogance is pride in action. The Bible is very clear about what happens when we are prideful and arrogant.

God wants us to draw near to Him. We cannot give credit to God if we take credit for ourselves for all that we have. Hence, pride draws us away from God, as the psalmist shows us:

> In his pride the wicked man does not seek him;
>   in all his thoughts there is no room for God
> (Psalm 10:4, NIV).

What about how we associate with others when we have a spirit of pride within? How does pride affect our everyday lives? Proverbs has something to say about this as well:

> Pride leads to conflict;
>   those who take advice are wise
> (Proverbs 13:10, NLT).

Point-blank, pride leads to conflict. Are you ever around someone arrogant and prideful? A prideful friend, coworker, boss, or teacher? How do you feel about them? How does their behavior make you feel about yourself? Pride creates both external and internal conflict.

The word "conflict" in Proverbs 13:10 is translated from the Hebrew word *matstsah*, which means:

Contention: striving against opposition.

Pride is self-deception. God addresses this as well in Obadiah's vision from the Lord:

> The LORD says to Edom,
> "I will cut you down to size among the nations;
>   you will be greatly despised.
> You have been deceived by your own pride
>   because you live in a rock fortress
>   and make your home high in the mountains.
> 'Who can ever reach us way up here?'
>   you ask boastfully.
> But even if you soar as high as eagles
>   and build your nest among the stars,
> I will bring you crashing down,"
>   says the LORD (Obadiah 1:2-4, NLT).

The Edomites were the descendants of Jacob's brother Esau; they were rough and daring mountaineers. They lived in a rock fortress in Sela, today known as Petra, in southern Jordan. Petra's ancient ruins are still a testament to the magnificent city it once was. The Edomites were immensely proud of their achievements, but God ultimately brought them down as promised. They were overrun by the Nabatean Arabs in the fifth century BC, which led to their removal from Sela.[c] Yes, the Edomites were self-deceived and believed that they were untouchable.

Sixty-one Bible verses address pride negatively; these references are mainly found in the prophets and the books of poetry.

Here are a few more to look at on your own: 1 Samuel 17:28, Proverbs 14:3, Proverbs 15:25, Proverbs 16:5, Proverbs 21:4, Proverbs 21:24, Proverbs 29:23, Proverbs 30:11-13, Proverbs 30:32, Jeremiah 49:16, Jeremiah 50:31, Jeremiah 50:32, Daniel 5:20, and 1 Peter 5:5.

Pride is dangerous; it's also hard to recognize in ourselves. We are typically unaware when we have a high opinion of ourselves. Our opinions seem valid to us. The proud also tend to have an attitude that credits themselves for success and blames others for failures.

Signs of Spiritual Pride

Jonathan Edwards, an eighteenth-century revivalist preacher, philosopher, and theologian, wrote about spiritual pride.[d] Let's examine signs of spiritual pride to self-evaluate.

1. Finding Faults

The proud find faults with others. The proud filter out God's goodness in others and only see their faults. Do we find ourselves criticizing others? Why do we criticize? The proud tend to criticize others when they see them doing something differently from what they would do or agree with. This criticism may not be related to someone else committing a sin, but rather, it may be about a task. For instance, it could be the way they dress, the way they manage their finances, the way they take care of their home, or the way they discipline their children. Essentially, by criticizing this way, we indirectly imply that our way is better.

2. Having a Harsh Spirit

The proud display a harsh spirit when they speak of others' sins with contempt, irritation, frustration, or judgment. Remember Jesus' words from John:

> So when they continued asking Him, He raised Himself up and said to them, "He who is without sin among you, let him throw a stone at her first" (John 8:7, NKJV).

Yes, we should address a fellow believer's sin privately, not openly and publicly. We are not to condemn them; we are to restore them. Paul tells us:

> Brothers and sisters, if someone is caught in a sin, you who live by the Spirit should restore that person gently. But watch yourselves, or you also may be tempted (Galatians 6:1, NIV).

Regarding judging, we can speak out against sins God condemns, such as lying, stealing, and adultery. However, we should be cautious when passing judgment based on personal convictions that God does not explicitly condemn. As Christians, we are convicted by the Holy Spirit not to do certain things; these are the things that are detrimental to us specifically. If we go against what the Holy Spirit has impressed upon us, we are committing a sin. However, just because it's a sin for us does not necessarily make it a sin for others. That is between them and God. Remember, I am *not* talking about those things condemned by God in the Bible.

There are many Scriptures where the Holy Spirit impressed upon a specific person or group of people to do or not to do something. For example, Paul, Silas, and Timothy "were forbidden by the Holy Spirit to preach the word in Asia" (Acts 16:6, NKJV). Being forbidden to preach the word in Asia isn't a command for all; it was specific to them at that time. Had they gone into Asia and preached the word, they would have sinned.

We also cannot judge someone's motives. We don't know their heart; only God knows the heart. We also cannot judge someone's eternal fate. Yes, if they are not believers in Jesus Christ, they will spend eternity in Hell; however, only God truly knows one's heart.

3. Being Shallow

The spiritually proud are shallow. They are much more concerned with how others view them on the outside rather than the reality of their hearts. The proud are concerned about what people know about them and strive to make those areas appear good. But the hidden secrets that no one knows about, the proud have little concern for. They consider them acceptable as long as no one else knows. Being shallow can lead to a spirit of human, earthly perfectionism. Instead, we should strive to be like Christ rather than seeking to please man with our earthly perfection. Paul's attitude is an excellent example for us when he wrote:

> Obviously, I'm not trying to win the approval
> of people, but of God. If pleasing people

99

were my goal, I would not be Christ's servant (Galatians 1:10, NLT).

If our goal is to please man, we are not Christ's servants; hence, we don't belong to Him. Focus on pleasing God; man will have difficulty finding legitimate fault with you.

4. Being Easily Offended

The proud become offended and defensive with challenges or corrections. A person with a defensive spirit is overly concerned with guarding against criticism. They tend to see an offense where none was intended, and they are on the defensive, always trying to justify their actions. On the other hand, the humble choose their battles from the attacks of others. Like the humble, we are to continue doing what God would have us to do, standing firm and aligning ourselves with God's word. Satan wants to put us on the defensive. If we are always defensive, we are not relying on God—we have pushed God out of the picture.

5. Having Self-Confidence Before God

There are two sides to self-confidence before God. In Christ, we can approach God with humble assurance. As we approach God, if we are missing either of these two components— humility or assurance—pride may be the issue. We are told in Hebrews that we can boldly approach the throne of God:

> Let us therefore come boldly to the throne of grace, that we may obtain mercy and find grace to help in time of need (Hebrews 4:16, NKJV).

However, we must be cautious and not forget that He is God. We cannot have so much assurance and boldness that we forget who we are in relation to God. We are to always approach God with humility, reverence, and respect.

Some people lack confidence before God, which may seem like humility but is another sign of pride. We lack assurance and doubt God if we believe our sins are greater than His grace. Now, we are pushing God out and relying upon ourselves; we subconsciously take the attitude that we don't need God or that He is not enough.

6. Being Desperate for Attention

Pride strongly desires attention and respect. Do we seek glory from man? The spiritually proud want everyone to look at them; they want to be in control and the center of attention. Do we desire material possessions and notoriety to receive recognition from others? During Jesus' ministry, there were some among the leaders who believed in Him, but because of the Pharisees, they didn't openly acknowledge their faith because they were afraid of being put out of the synagogue. Unfortunately, they loved human praise more than praise from God (John 12:42-43). Strive to please God, desperately seeking Him rather than man.

7. Overlooking Others

Pride often leads people to favor some individuals over others. Those who are proud desire to associate themselves with those in positions of authority and power and seek recognition from such individuals. They consciously, or maybe even unconsciously, overlook the weak, the inconvenient, or the unattractive because they don't believe these individuals can offer them much. They focus on what they can gain from others rather than what they can do for them.

Jesus teaches the opposite; it's more about what we can do for others. We should help others without expecting anything in return. The book of Proverbs tells us what God will do when we are helpful or when we ignore those in need:

> Being kind to the poor is like lending to the LORD;
>   he will reward you for what you have done
> (Proverbs 19:17, NCV).

Conversely,

> Those who shut their ears to the cries of the poor
>   will be ignored in their own time of need
> (Proverbs 21:13, NLT).

Help those in need without expecting them to return the favor. Give and help from the heart; God will see what you have done. When helping others, remember not to go around bragging about what you have done. Don't strive for recognition from man; if you do, you will have already received your reward here on Earth, as Jesus tells us in Matthew:

> "Watch out! Don't do your good deeds publicly, to be admired by others, for you will lose the reward from your Father in heaven. When you give to someone in need, don't do as the hypocrites do—blowing trumpets in

the synagogues and streets to call attention to their acts of charity! I tell you the truth, they have received all the reward they will ever get. But when you give to someone in need, don't let your left hand know what your right hand is doing. Give your gifts in private, and your Father, who sees everything, will reward you" (Matthew 6:1-4, NLT).

God will also see what you haven't done when you have the opportunity.

Seriously, self-reflect on these things. If you are honest with yourself, do you fall into any of the categories? I know I do. Yes, we all have pride to some degree; that is human nature. However, human nature isn't an excuse. Search your heart and ask God to show you areas in your life where you fall into pride and are genuinely unaware. The antidote to pride is humility. The chapter on humility, Chapter 11, is the perfect place to start as you strive to overcome the sin that God absolutely hates.

Is All Pride Sinful?

Let's tackle a big question—is all pride considered evil or sinful? What about when we say we are proud of our child's accomplishments or the achievement of a successful project to help the homeless? Is it wrong to feel proud of these things? What if we work hard at our jobs and have thriving careers? Is it wrong to take pride in our achievements? Remembering and recognizing who gave us the desire and ability to accomplish our tasks is important.

The ultimate question is, are we looking inwardly at ourselves or outwardly to God and others? The pride that God condemns throughout the Bible is self-pride. Celebrating an accomplishment is okay, but we need to be careful and not let it lead to self-pride. Do this by remembering where your success comes from: your Heavenly Father. Once again, it's a heart issue. Where is your heart—looking inward or outward, taking all the credit or giving credit and thanks to God?

Proverbs gives us an example of *good* pride:

> Grandchildren are the pride and joy of old
> men and a son is proud of his father
> (Proverbs 17:6, NLV).

When we raise our children according to God's plans and see them raising their children in God's ways, we feel proud, bringing us true joy. We are proud because our grandchildren are walking with God, and as a result, their life on this Earth will be one of faith and hope. Plus, we take comfort in knowing our grandchildren will spend eternity with God. It's the same with a child when godly parents lead the home in a loving and nurturing way. As that child becomes an adult, they can reflect on their childhood and are proud (and grateful) of their parents and the home they were provided and raised in.

Another example is Paul writing to the church in Corinth:

> I trust you and am proud of you. You give me
> much comfort and joy even when I suffer
> (2 Corinthians 7:4, NLT).

Paul had sent Titus to Corinth to serve the church there. Titus later returned to Macedonia and reported the status of the church in Corinth to Paul. In this passage, Paul commends the Corinthians for their repentance and how they welcomed and encouraged Titus.

Both examples demonstrate looking outwardly to others and feeling a positive sense of pride.

Pride is the devil's sin. The first sin ever committed. God absolutely hates pride. Pride draws us away from God and leads to ingratitude and destruction. The proud push God aside because they think they don't need Him; they can do it themselves. The proud are controlling and cause both internal and external conflict to those around them. We can easily fall into the sin of pride and not realize it. Self-reflect on the subtle signs of pride: finding faults, having a harsh spirit, being shallow, being easily offended, having self-confidence before God, being desperate for attention, and overlooking others.

Pride is a heart issue. Are we looking inwardly at ourselves or outwardly to God? Do we put God and others before ourselves? Not all pride is sinful; always credit God for all things. Recognizing the blessings God has given you will help keep your pride in check.

We cannot believe God's grace
is sufficient until
we believe we are insufficient

The thorns given to us
are meant to make us stronger

CHAPTER 8

Thorns

What is a thorn? We all experience them, either temporarily or continuously. A thorn is something that nags at us, and we want to eliminate it. In the literal sense, a thorn is a stiff, sharp-pointed, straight, or curved woody projection on the stem or other part of a plant[a], and it hurts when it sticks into our skin. Metaphorically, a thorn is anything that repeatedly annoys or causes problems. It can be a health issue, a problematic situation, or a challenging circumstance. A thorn can also be a person, such as a family member, a neighbor, a teacher, a co-worker, a boss, or a client.

I have a thorn; it's called scoliosis. I have severe scoliosis. I was diagnosed at thirteen and experience pain daily. Very few people around me know that I have this condition. Why is that? Mostly because I don't complain. However, I pray about it daily. I ask God not to allow my condition to worsen and to let my spine function so that I can do the things I need to do and enjoy doing. I ask Him to take away the continual pain and allow me to sleep peacefully at night.

Yes, I pray and proactively work on my condition daily. I know that anything positive concerning my condition is entirely by God's grace, not what I do. However, I cannot sit and wallow in my situation. I have to give God something to work with: positivity and action. I get up early every morning and spend one and a half hours stretching and doing exercises designed for my condition. Then, I do additional stretches and exercises throughout the day. Yes, I have severe scoliosis. Yes, I am in pain daily. Yes, God is in complete control of my condition. Yes, God is good! Yes, I am blessed!

Baseball great Lou Gehrig[b] had a thorn. He played Major League Baseball for seventeen seasons. He was renowned for his prowess as a hitter and for his durability, earning his nickname "The Iron Horse." Gehrig played in 2,130 consecutive games for the Yankees, a significant accomplishment. He was inducted into the Baseball Hall of Fame in 1939. That same year, Lou Gehrig was diagnosed with a neuromuscular disease called amyotrophic lateral sclerosis, or ALS—later known as "Lou Gehrig's Disease." He passed away just two years later. ALS has no cure, and the life expectancy after diagnosis is usually two to five years. Lou Gehrig made one of the most famous speeches in sports history on July 4, 1939, at Yankee Stadium on Lou Gehrig Appreciation Day. He began his speech with these memorable words:

> For the past two weeks, you have been reading
> about a bad break. Yet today, I consider myself
> the luckiest man on the face of the earth.[c]

He went on to say why he was lucky. We cannot always control the cards we are dealt in life, but we choose how to play them and our attitude toward them. Lou Gehrig had a thorn with no cure, no chance of reversal, and a short time to live. Yet, he looked at the blessings in his life.

Do you know who else had a thorn? Paul—the greatest apostle who walked the face of the earth, brought the gospel of Jesus Christ to the Gentiles, and wrote thirteen of the twenty-seven books in the New Testament (some scholars believe he wrote fifteen).

Paul spoke of his thorn in 2 Corinthians:

> Because of the extraordinary greatness of the revelations, for this reason, to keep me from exalting myself, there was given to me a thorn in the flesh, a messenger of Satan to torment me—to keep me from exalting myself! Concerning this I pleaded with the Lord three times that it might leave me. And He has said to me, "My grace is sufficient for you, for power is perfected in weakness." Most gladly, therefore, I will rather boast about my weaknesses, so that the power of Christ may dwell in me. Therefore I delight in weaknesses, in insults, in distresses, in persecutions, in difficulties, in behalf of Christ; for when I am weak, then I am strong (2 Corinthians 12:7-10, NASB).

The word "thorn" is translated from the Greek word *skólops*, which means:

> Properly, anything with a sharp point, a thorn, (figuratively) an instrument producing pain or discomfort (acute irritation).

It's interesting to note that the word *skólops* is only used in this passage. In all other instances where the word "thorn" is mentioned in the Bible, it refers to a prickly plant, an actual thorn bush.

Paul states that the thorn was delivered by "a messenger of Satan to torment [him]." The word "torment" in the original Greek text is the word *kolaphizó,* which means:

> Properly, to strike with the fist (literally "knuckles"); to hit hard "with the knuckles," to make the blow sting and crush.

Satan struck Paul. Satan delivered the thorn; God allowed Satan to inflict Paul.

God's Grace

Why did God allow Paul's thorn? Paul tells us it was to "keep [him] from exalting [himself]." Paul had a tendency towards pride. Paul received extraordinary revelations from God, which could have easily led to pride. Through his thorn, Paul saw and experienced God's grace. Paul saw that when he was weak, he was strong in Christ. Because of the great revelations given to Paul, God needed to keep Paul from exhibiting spiritual pride, hence the thorn.

Perhaps the thorns we experience serve the same purpose: to prevent us from falling into a particular sin we are entirely unaware of. God may use a thorn in our lives to make us aware that we are inadequate without Him. We need God's power to be active in our lives and to realize that He is enough. We need to depend and rely upon Him entirely.

Paul pleaded with God three times, and God gave him an answer. It was not the answer he wanted, but it was an answer, nonetheless. After that, Paul didn't ask God again; he had his answer. God wanted Paul to fully rely upon Him. When we depend upon God's grace, we give Him all the glory. God's answer to Paul's prayer was that His grace was sufficient; Paul could bear his thorn through God's grace. Paul's response showed how he accepted God's answer. His situation didn't change; the thorn was still there, but Paul embraced God's response in faith.

Grace. We keep discussing grace, but what is God's grace? In the New Testament, one-hundred and fifty-seven passages use the word "grace" which is translated from the Greek word *charis* and means:

> Grace, as a gift or blessing brought to man by
> Jesus Christ, favor, gratitude, thanks, a favor,
> kindness.

Simply put, grace is an undeserved gift. Specifically, in 2 Corinthians 12:9, when God told Paul, "'My grace is sufficient for you,'" it means:

The favor of Christ, assisting and strengthening his followers and ministers to bear their troubles.

When we receive God's grace, we recognize God's approval of us. Grace is given freely and cannot be taken away. When we stumble, God's grace is there. I like how Charles Spurgeon talked about grace:

It is easy to believe in grace for the past and the future, but to rest in it for the immediate necessity is true faith. Believer, it is now that grace is sufficient: even at this moment, it is enough for thee.[d]

Strength in Weakness

So, what was Paul's thorn? We don't know. Scripture doesn't tell us. God had a reason for not revealing Paul's thorn. If God had revealed what the thorn was, others with a thorn, but not the same thorn as Paul, may doubt that Paul's experience applied to them. What Paul's thorn was does not matter. What matters is God's purpose for the thorn. God wants all who have a thorn in the flesh to relate to Paul and embrace that in our weakness, we are made strong if we fully rely upon God. God said, "My grace is sufficient for you." He didn't say, "For you, Paul." God kept the statement open and broad to include all of us. There can be no mistake; God was not just talking about His grace for Paul but for all of us. Yes, you and me.

Are you ever desperate to find relief from a burden, a heavy weight, a thorn? There are two ways to alleviate a burden.

Firstly, by removing the load, or secondly, by strengthening the back that bears the load. Instead of taking away a thorn, God strengthens us under it. By doing this, He shows His strength through our weakness.

For this to work in our lives, we need to believe God's grace is sufficient. We cannot believe God's grace is sufficient until we believe we are insufficient.[e] Many of us are too strong for God to use us. We tend to be self-reliant. Being independent is something I have personally struggled with. I can do it myself; I don't need help. We cannot receive strength through God until we truly realize our weakness.

Paul realized that he could not remove his thorn; he was insufficient. Once Paul realized that he was insufficient, he pled to God, and God told Paul that His grace was sufficient. Once Paul received and embraced this, he could move on and be strong. We will receive the sufficiency of God's grace when we acknowledge our insufficiency.

Who Are We

When we have a thorn, it shows us who we truly are in Christ. A thorn unveils us; it pulls away the layers like an onion. Who are we deep down? Are we who we profess to be? A thorn makes us examine ourselves, our thoughts, our beliefs, and our reliance upon God. A thorn takes us to the core of who we are. Yes, we are human; we have weak moments. However, where do we firmly stand? Do we truly believe God is who He says He is? Do we truly believe that God is faithful? Do we truly believe that God is sufficient? Once again, God may not remove our thorns, but if we recognize our inadequacies and turn fully to Him, He will walk us in and through our thorns.

We all have thorns. View thorns as guidance, not punishment from God.[f] Thorns get our attention; a thorn can transform us and our relationship with God. Thorns are not meant to defeat us; thorns are not meant to make us weaker. The thorns given to us are meant to make us stronger. Thorns are intended to strengthen us through reliance and dependence upon God.

Find the positive in the thorn. It's hard to do, but if we allow the thorn to transform us, we can look back and be grateful for the positives that came from it.

PART THREE

SWEEPING DIRT

True joy rises
above our circumstances

We often see things not as they are
but as we are

CHAPTER 9

Finding the Positive

How do we find ways to thank God daily? Let's begin by expressing gratitude to God for the things around us that we may easily take for granted. Even on a typical day, there are numerous things to be grateful for. Here are some of the things I am thankful for:

> A safe home that is environmentally controlled. When I go to bed at night, I don't fear for my safety.

> A car that gets me to and from work. I am thankful for the vehicle, the job, and the opportunity to learn and grow professionally.

> A family that loves me and, more importantly, loves God.

> The privilege to openly and publicly gather for worship with fellow believers each week without fear.

The beautiful sunrise and sunset; rain for the nourishment of our soil.

God loves me, He loves my family, and He has given us eternal life with Him. His enormous sacrifice of His Son. For being a loving and just God full of mercy and grace.

It's amazing how many blessings surround me every day, both big and small. I encourage you to take some time to reflect on the things you are grateful for and to express your heartfelt thanks to God. It's easy to take things for granted, so let's consciously thank Him each day for the things we easily overlook.

Joy

Always be joyful. Never stop praying. Be thankful in all circumstances, for this is God's will for you who belong to Christ Jesus (1 Thessalonians 5:16-18, NLT).

When Paul wrote this to the Thessalonians, they lived with harsh daily persecution. Paul encouraged the believers at Thessalonica to "be joyful" even in dire circumstances.

Paul also uses the word "always." We cannot constantly carry joy in our lives if we look at the circumstances of life. We need to understand the difference between joy and happiness.

Happiness is contingent on circumstances. I'm happy after a pay raise. I'm unhappy after failing an exam.

What is joy? Fifty-nine passages in the New Testament use the word "joy," which is translated from the Greek word *chara* and means:

> Properly, the awareness (of God's) grace, favor;
> joy ("grace recognized").

Joy is the recognition of God's grace. True joy rises above our circumstances. True joy is a peace within your heart that only the Holy Spirit can provide. Joy comes from within the soul regardless of circumstances. Our joy depends on our orientation to God's providence and promises. God's providence is the way He arranges things to achieve His sovereign purpose. Know that God is in complete and absolute control of every aspect of our lives. If we know God's promises and we see God's faithfulness in our lives, we can find joy, even when times are not good. Life is hard, and we all have times or seasons when things are not going well. Paul demonstrated this unlike any other. The Romans imprisoned Paul twice. 2 Corinthians tells of other things he endured:

> Five different times the Jewish leaders gave me thirty-nine lashes. Three times I was beaten with rods. Once I was stoned. Three times I was shipwrecked. Once I spent a whole night and a day adrift at sea. I have traveled on many long journeys. I have faced danger from rivers and from robbers. I have faced danger from my own people, the Jews, as well as from the Gentiles. I have faced danger in the cities, in the deserts, and on the seas. And

I have faced danger from men who claim to be believers but are not. I have worked hard and long, enduring many sleepless nights. I have been hungry and thirsty and have often gone without food. I have shivered in the cold without enough clothing to keep me warm (2 Corinthians 11:24-27, NLT).

Verse 24 emphasizes thirty-nine lashes. Why thirty-nine? According to the Old Testament law, forty lashes was the most that could be given (Deuteronomy 24:3). The Jews would give no more than thirty-nine lashes for fear of accidentally breaking the law. Although beaten to an inch of his life on five occasions, Paul remained full of joy.

Be Positive

We often see things not as they are but as we are. When we feel depressed, overwhelmed, or discouraged, our perspective often becomes distorted and disconnected from reality. Every day may not be good, but we need to consciously find something good in every day. Finding the positive in a negative situation may require a conscious and decisive effort, especially if you are not naturally inclined to do so. However, by consistently having this mindset, it can become second nature. Whenever you encounter a negative situation in your life, which is inevitable, take a moment to step back, take a deep breath, and try to find something positive about it. Similarly, at the end of a long and challenging day, take a moment to reflect and find something positive that happened that day. When my daughter was younger, I would ask her to share the best part of her day as

I put her to bed. Sometimes, she would also tell me something about her day that made her sad. We would discuss it and try to find something positive in it. As parents and grandparents, we can teach our children and grandchildren to focus on the good things in their lives regardless of age.

A quote often attributed to Abraham Lincoln that I like is:

> We can complain because rose bushes have thorns, or rejoice because thorn bushes have roses.

Being positive is a choice; being negative is a choice. The choice is yours. Find the positive.

Thankful in All Circumstances

How can we be thankful in all circumstances? What about when things are not going well? What do we do then? Thank God. No, I don't mean to thank Him for the bad things that are going on; find the good amongst the bad, and thank Him for His hand in your current situation. Thank Him for being in control of the outcome; thank Him for walking with you through the fire. Here is an excellent example of thanking God in a horrible situation.

Betsie ten Boom has the most incredible story about thankfulness and finding the positive.[a] Betsie and her sister, Corrie ten Boom, were Dutch Christians. During the Holocaust in World War II, Betsie and her family hid Jews in their home to help them escape the Nazis. They were caught and arrested.

Betsie and Corrie were sent to Ravensbruck concentration camp.

Betsie and Corrie lived in cramped, unsanitary, flea-infested quarters. Betsie always found the positive. In her prayers, she even thanked God for the fleas. Corrie struggled with thanking God for fleas of all things, but Betsie, quoting God's word, quickly reminded her:

"'Give thanks in all circumstances,' she quoted. It doesn't say, 'in pleasant circumstances.' Fleas are part of this place where God has put us."

Each day, after an eleven-hour labor-intensive work detail, Corrie and Betsie would hold Bible studies with the other prisoners, which was forbidden. The guards never came into their barracks and discovered what they were doing. They later realized the guards left them alone because they refused to enter the flea-infested barracks. God blessed them through the fleas.

Sometimes, we don't understand or like the situation or circumstance we're in. Give it to God. Pray and find things in your circumstances to thank Him for. He sees things from an eagle's eye view. He sees things we are entirely unaware of. Remember, He is working in our circumstances. He worked in Betsie and Corrie's circumstances through the fleas. What tremendous faith and courage they displayed. What a blessing they received. Thank God for the fleas!

I enjoy it when people share their stories of God's faithfulness. Share how God has blessed you and how He has shown His faithfulness.

Attitude Is a Choice

Viktor Frankl was a Jewish Austrian Holocaust survivor.[b] He spent three years in four different concentration camps. During this time, he lost his parents, brother, and wife, who were also in concentration camps. Released in 1945, Viktor Frankl wrote his famous book, *Man's Search for Meaning*, in a mere nine days in 1946. In his book, Mr. Frankl makes many profound statements. One of my favorites is:

> Everything can be taken from a man but one thing: the last of the human freedoms— to choose one's attitude in any given set of circumstances, to choose one's own way.

Attitude. In any circumstance, we can choose how to respond and move forward. Never let any person, situation, or circumstance take that away from you. You choose your attitude, so choose a positive one.

In my own life, God showed His faithfulness, and I learned to give thanks throughout a difficult situation. My eighty-year-old mother was diagnosed with cancer. After being diagnosed, she passed within six months. In the beginning, we were encouraged that she could be healed. We thanked God for His hand upon the situation and for giving us comfort. As time passed, it was evident that she would not survive. It was a rough road for all of us to witness what she was enduring. I thanked God for the godly mother He gave me and that I had her in my life for over fifty years. I thanked Him for her love and dedication to our family. I thanked Him for her life and what she meant to us. I thanked Him for giving my parents sixty-two years of marriage. I thanked Him for receiving her into His kingdom. Although it was an incredibly hard, sad time, I searched for the "good" and thanked God.

Cheerful Heart

Solomon tells us it also does something within us when we are positive:

> A cheerful heart is good medicine,
>   but a crushed spirit dries up the bones
> (Proverbs 17:22, NIV).

A cheerful heart or crushed spirit is a choice! This choice has nothing to do with fate, temperament, genetics, or health. This choice isn't the result of circumstances; a cheerful person can choose to find joy in horrible difficulties, and a gloomy person can ruin a remarkable event. Solomon also tells us we can have a continual feast through life if we have a joyful heart, but a person with a negative attitude always finds something wrong (Proverbs 15:15).

When someone is positive, one can see it in their countenance; the same is true with a negative person. Have you ever entered a room and noticed the positivity all over someone's face without knowing them? A person's demeanor isn't only shown through their speech but also their countenance. Our speech reflects what is in our hearts, and so does our countenance. Solomon tells us in Ecclesiastes:

> Who is like the wise?
> Who knows the explanation of things?

> A person's wisdom brightens their face
>   and changes its hard appearance
> (Ecclesiastes 8:1, NIV).

Wisdom is discerning and doing the preferred will of God. As we pursue God and discover His character, our hearts change, and it shows on our faces.

While Paul sat in Rome undergoing his first Roman imprisonment, he wrote to the church at Ephesus. The book of Ephesians deals with topics at the very core of what it means to be a Christian—both in faith and practice—regardless of any particular problem we face. Paul, while in prison, writes about our speech:

> Do not let any unwholesome talk come out
> of your mouths, but only what is helpful for
> building others up according to their needs,
> that it may benefit those who listen
> (Ephesians 4:29, NIV).

Would you rather be around someone who speaks positively and builds others up, or rather be around someone who is primarily negative and tears down? A negative person brings those around them down. Don't be that person. What does Jesus say about evil, negative speech? He tells us in Matthew:

> "You snakes! You are evil people! How can
> you say anything good? The mouth speaks the
> things that are in the heart. A good person has
> good things in his heart. And so he speaks the
> good things that come from his heart. But an

evil person has evil in his heart. So he speaks
the evil things that come from his heart"
(Matthew 12:34-35, ICB).

Our speech reveals what is in our hearts and exposes the
character of our hearts. Where do we spend our time? Do we
fill our hearts with good things or evil things? What kind of
music do we listen to? What kind of websites do we go to?
What kind of books do we read? What kind of people do we
hang out with? If we surround ourselves with what is good,
good will naturally come out of our mouths. Of course, the
opposite is true if we surround ourselves with that which isn't
good (evil). Remember, our body acts in the way in which our
soul directs it. Does our soul get filled with the world, or does
our soul get filled with the Holy Spirit? What goes in ultimately
comes out. Jesus goes on to say in verse 37:

"The words you have said will be used to judge
you. Some of your words will prove you right,
but some of your words will prove you guilty"
(Matthew 12:37, ICB).

Jesus tells us that our words will judge us. Will we be justified
or condemned? We need to surround ourselves with good; if
something bad comes along and we are hurting or mistreated,
we need to dig deep. Remember God's word and promises,
always find the positive, and let the words flow from our
mouths.

Physical Benefits

As an added plus, being positive also has health benefits. Medical studies confirm this fact taught by Solomon 3,000 years ago. Those who laugh and enjoy life will live longer. The Mayo Clinic[c] has identified several health benefits that positive thinking can provide, including:

- Increased lifespan
- Lower rates of depression
- Lower levels of distress
- Greater resistance to the common cold
- Better psychological and physical wellbeing
- Better cardiovascular health and reduced risk of death from cardiovascular disease
- Better coping skills during hardships and times of stress

———————•●———————

Nobody's life is free from pain and heartache. But we have a God who loves us and is in complete control. No, things don't always turn out as we would like. We lose homes, jobs, and loved ones and experience setbacks. However, it's crucial to find the positive. Sometimes, it's hard, but find the good and thank God for that good. Ask God to show you and help you see the good. Thank God that He is in control, already knows the outcome, and is working, although we may not see it. Attitude is a choice; strive to have a good one! Find the positive.

All disciples of Christ are Christians
but not all Christians are disciples

CHAPTER 10

Living Sacrifice

What is the definition of a disciple? The basic definition is someone who adheres to the teachings of another.[a] A disciple is a follower or a learner. Starting with that definition, what is a disciple of Jesus Christ? Yes, there were the original disciples who learned and followed Jesus's teachings while He was on Earth. Today, what does it mean to be a disciple, a disciple of Jesus Christ?

All disciples of Christ are Christians, but not all Christians are disciples. A disciple lives for Christ and follows His teachings. A true disciple denies himself of earthly temptations and pleasures and does what Christ would have him do. A true disciple lives in this world but isn't of this world; a true disciple reflects the values of Heaven in the decisions they make. A true disciple shares the word of Jesus. Do we fail at being a disciple? Yes, every day. Strive to keep your focus on Christ, know Him, know His character, know His teachings, and follow Him.

After His resurrection, Jesus spent time with His disciples on the Mount of Olives. This is the same place where He ascended into Heaven and where He will return one day. Jesus gave His disciples the great commission on this mountain.

> "Therefore, go and make disciples of all the nations, baptizing them in the name of the Father and the Son and the Holy Spirit. Teach these new disciples to obey all the commands I have given you. And be sure of this: I am with you always, even to the end of the age" (Matthew 28:19-20, NLT).

In Matthew 28:20, Jesus tells us He is with us always, even to the end of the age. He didn't say, "I *will be* with you." He said, "I *am* with you." Jesus, the living son of God, the one who is all and who knows all, the one whom the demons tremble at His name, the one who healed the sick and made the blind see and the lame walk, and the one who rose from the dead, He—is—with—us! Jesus is with us until the end of the age, the time until Christ's return.

Before His crucifixion, Jesus told His disciples what it takes to be His disciple:

> Then Jesus said to his disciples, "Whoever wants to be my disciple must deny themselves and take up their cross and follow me. For whoever wants to save their life [or soul] will lose it, but whoever loses their life for me will find it. What good will it be for someone to gain the whole world, yet forfeit their soul?

> Or what can anyone give in exchange for their soul? For the Son of Man is going to come in his Father's glory with his angels, and then he will reward each person according to what they have done" (Matthew 16:24-27, NIV).

First, we must *want* to be Jesus' disciples. To *want* is to *desire*. Have a desire to be His disciple, to follow Him. No one is forced to follow Jesus; God gave us all free will. We follow Jesus because we want to; we desire to.

Jesus said we must deny ourselves. Jesus is instructing us to deny what our flesh wants, the desires of the flesh that go against God's teachings. It becomes easier as we deny self and keep our focus on Jesus. I said easier, not easy. We all have our weak moments. When you fail in a particular area of life, ask God for forgiveness, let Him pick you up, and continue to strive to keep your focus on Jesus.

So, let's further examine Jesus' words. What did He mean when He said, "'Take up their cross'"? In this passage, according to *Strong's Concordance*, "'take up their cross'" means:

> Used by those who, on behalf of God's cause, do not hesitate cheerfully and manfully to bear persecutions, troubles, distresses—thus recalling the fate of Christ and the spirit in which he encountered it.

In other words, no matter the cost, follow Him. If we are persecuted, made fun of, or mistreated because of Jesus, follow Him anyway. Deny ourselves of what the world says and follow what Jesus says. Remember who the current ruler of this world is—Satan. The world promotes lying, stealing, foul language, drunkenness, and drug use, among other things. Jesus says to follow His teachings.

In the New Testament, Jesus said, "'Take up your cross and follow me'" five times (Matthew 10:38, Matthew 16:25, Mark 8:34, Luke 9:23, Luke 14:27).

How do we follow Jesus? First and foremost, we worship Him and Him alone. Worship is recognizing Jesus for who He is, what He has done, and what we are trusting Him to do.

We worship by reading the Bible and following Jesus' teachings. We can only follow His teachings if we read and study His word; we cannot follow what we don't know. Sing praises to His name and exalt Him. Don't be embarrassed or ashamed to speak of and praise Him to others. Talk to God in prayer through Jesus. All these things build a relationship with Him. This sounds easy, but the critical point is that we are to worship Him and Him alone. Worship is to be done with joy, not begrudgingly. Worship must come from the heart. I understand that sometimes we don't feel like worshiping; we are going through a difficult time, overwhelmed with problems, and stressed out. During these times, we need to worship Him anyway.

This particular passage concerning taking up your cross captures my attention. In Matthew 10, Jesus says:

> "If you refuse to take up your cross and follow
> me, you are not worthy of being mine"
> (Matthew 10:38, NLT).

The phrase "not worthy" in the Greek translation means "not deserving." Wow, straight from Jesus' mouth. If you don't take up your cross and follow Jesus, you do *not deserve* Jesus. One day, I don't want Jesus to look at His Father and say those words about me, "She is not worthy." Powerful, powerful words.

Soul Saving

In Matthew 16:25, Jesus says, "'For whoever wants to save their life [or soul] will lose it, but whoever loses their life for me will find it'" (NIV). The word "life" means soul. Remember, the soul is the connection between the spirit and the body. Whoever wants to follow the world and save their soul in this life will lose it in the next life. Saving your soul in the physical world will cause you to lose it in the spiritual. Give up worldliness, give up following the world for Jesus, and you will find your life in Heaven one day. Once again, the soul tells the body what to do. So, does our soul listen to the world and direct our bodies accordingly, or does our soul listen to the Holy Spirit and direct our bodies to do as Christ would have us do? For the Holy Spirit to direct our bodies, we must invite the Holy Spirit into our lives by accepting Jesus Christ as our Savior. If you are a Christian, you will spend eternity in Heaven. The question is, are you going to bring a little bit of Heaven to Earth? Will you follow Jesus as His disciple and receive blessings while here on Earth?

In Matthew 16:26, Jesus asks, "'What good is it to gain the whole world yet forfeit their soul?'" When we gain the whole world, we possess it for all its riches and pleasures. If we strive to gain the world, we give up our souls; we pay a price. If we live for this world, we will get our rewards in this world. Our worldly rewards are temporary, and all our self-gains in this world will result in loss in the next world. Don't value your temporary life here on Earth more than your eternal life. If we lose our souls (if we are not Christians), Hell offers no redemption. A soul isn't recoverable once judged and condemned to Hell. At this point, there are no second chances. Live for Christ while on Earth and receive your rewards in Heaven. Jesus, in verse 27, then goes on to tell us He is coming one day to give each his rewards according to what each has done.

Going Through the Motions

The Israelites gave their sacrifices to God; however, oftentimes, they went through the motions to check a box. In Psalm 50, God is rebuking His people, Israel. They became complacent with their sacrifices. God didn't rebuke them because of their sacrifice; He rebuked them because of their lack of thanksgiving:

> Not for your sacrifices do I rebuke you;
>   your burnt offerings are
>   continually before me
> (Psalm 50:8, ESV).

> You give your mouth free rein for evil,
>   and your tongue frames deceit.

You sit and speak against your brother;
　　you slander your own mother's son.
These things you have done,
and I have been silent;
　　you thought that I was one like yourself.
But now I rebuke you and lay
　　the charge before you
(Psalm 50:19-21, ESV).

As we live our lives as a living sacrifice, we want to please God. How do we please God with our sacrifice? Psalm 50 gives us insight:

Offer to God a sacrifice of thanksgiving,
　　and perform your vows to the Most High,
and call upon me in the day of trouble;
　　I will deliver you, and you shall glorify me
(Psalm 50:14-15, ESV).

The one who offers thanksgiving as his sacrifice glorifies me;
　　to one who orders his way rightly
　　I will show the salvation of God!
(Psalm 50:23, ESV).

When we genuinely give thanks from our hearts, we glorify God. He knows what lies in our hearts, and a sacrifice of thanksgiving is a living sacrifice for Him. We can go through the motions, like the Israelites did, and keep a checklist of our good deeds and acts of kindness. However, while we may be able to fool others or even ourselves, we cannot fool God. God wants sincerity in our hearts.

Discerner of Hearts

John shows us that Jesus is the discerner of all hearts:

> Now while he was in Jerusalem at the Passover Festival, many people saw the signs he was performing and believed in his name. But Jesus would not entrust himself to them, for he knew all people. He did not need any testimony about mankind, for he knew what was in each person (John 2:23-25, NIV).

Jesus does not relate to all Christians the same.[b] John 2:23 tells us many believed in His name. They were saved and would spend eternity in Heaven when they left this Earth. But verse 24 states that Jesus did not entrust Himself to them because He knew what was in them. Although saved, Jesus would not commit Himself to them. Why? Because they were not committed yet. They would go to Heaven one day, but Jesus could not use them here on Earth. Jesus wasn't ready to impart His authority to them. They were not "all in."

Sometimes, we may wonder why our prayers are not answered or why we don't see calm in the middle of our storms. The reason could be that Jesus doesn't see our full commitment to Him. We are able to change God's mind. God has an unconditional and conditional will; we see examples of this throughout Scripture (Exodus 32:14, Jeremiah 26:19, Amos 7:3). If God's will is conditional concerning a particular matter, we won't change His mind until we are committed to Him and through fervent prayer. We cannot water down Christianity to only be heavenly. We must live it out in all areas of our lives. Jesus knows our hearts. If our hearts aren't pure, a close relationship with Him won't exist. Remember, God will only answer prayers that align with His will. Jesus can use whomever He pleases—Christians, disciples, and non-Christians—but as a non-disciple, we miss out on so much on this side of Heaven.

Sacrifices That Please

What kind of sacrifices please God? The writer of Hebrews tells us:

> Through Jesus, therefore, let us continually offer to God a sacrifice of praise—the fruit of lips that openly profess his name. And do not forget to do good and to share with others, for with such sacrifices God is pleased (Hebrews 13:15-16, NIV).

Openly profess His name. Never be ashamed of Jesus. When we are married or have a close friend with whom we spend a lot of time, it's natural for their name to come up in conversation. Similarly, as we grow closer to Jesus, we tend to speak about Him more openly and profess His name without hesitation.

What else does the writer of Hebrews tell us about what pleases God? We are to do good and pass our blessings on to others. God blesses us with many things, including our health, family, peace, abilities, caring hearts, wisdom, education, and opportunities. When we share our blessings with others, the writer of Hebrews tells us, "With such sacrifices God is pleased." God is pleased when we sacrifice for others. God gave the ultimate sacrifice for us, His Son, on the cross. Being kind and helping others is the least we can do. When Jesus walked the face of this Earth as a man, He continually helped those in need. As His disciples, we are to do the same. In Ephesians, Paul reminds us of this.

> Therefore, be imitators of God as dear children. And walk in love, as Christ also has loved us and given Himself for us, an offering and a sacrifice to God for a sweet-smelling aroma (Ephesians 5:1-2, NKJV).

"Therefore" ties this verse to the previous verse:

> And be kind to one another, tenderhearted, forgiving one another, even as God in Christ forgave you (Ephesians 4:32, NKJV).

Be imitators of God. Ephesians 5 is the only place in the Bible where the word "imitate" is applied to the Christian in relation to God. This verse sums up the New Testament regarding our character and conduct. Be like God, imitate Him, be kind, tenderhearted, and forgiving. We are to be imitators of God because we are His children and are created in His image.

Spiritual Sacrifice

In the Old Testament, the people would come to the temple and present their offerings and blood sacrifices to the priest. The priest would take the sacrifices of the people and offer them up to God. Only the priests could present the sacrifices to God. The people came to the Father through the priest. Peter connects our role now to the role of the priests we read about in the Old Testament:

> You are coming to Christ, who is the living cornerstone of God's temple. He was rejected by people, but he was chosen by God for great honor. And you are living stones that God is building into his spiritual temple. What's more, you are his holy priests. Through the mediation of Jesus Christ, you offer spiritual sacrifices that please God
> (1 Peter 2:4-5, NLT).

In 1 Peter 2:4, Peter states that Christ is the living cornerstone of God's temple, then in verse 5, he says we are living stones that God is building into His spiritual temple. Jesus is the cornerstone, but we, as Christians, are built into the spiritual temple. What is the temple today? Our bodies. Paul tells us that our bodies are temples of the Holy Spirit, who is in us and whom we received from God, and we are not our own (1 Corinthians 6:19).

Before Christ, God dwelled in the temple. During the time of Moses, God dwelled in a portable temple, the Tabernacle. When the temple was built in Jerusalem, God dwelled there. That is why the Israelites would go to the temple with their blood sacrifices. After the death of Christ, God, through the Holy Spirit, dwells in each of us as Christians.

Peter tells us that we are God's holy priests. What does that mean? We can boldly approach God's throne of grace without going through an intermediary. Through Christ, we can go directly to God at any time. There are no longer any barriers.

Now, what does Peter tell us about the sacrifice given in the temple (now our bodies) by the priests (now us)? We are to give spiritual sacrifices—ourselves. Give our all to God; present our best to Him. Peter took the laws of the Old Testament and related them to Christians today. We have so much freedom due to the ultimate sacrifice of Christ on the cross. We can freely go to the Father and have an intimate personal conversation with Him. He dwells within us; He is always with us. That leads to the question, "Are we always with Him?" Do we honor Him with our bodies and our spiritual sacrifices?

Paul sums it all up in Romans:

> And so, dear brothers and sisters, I plead with you to give your bodies to God because of all he has done for you. Let them be a living and holy sacrifice—the kind he will find acceptable. This is truly the way to worship him. Don't copy the behavior and customs of this world, but let God transform you into a new person by changing the way you think. Then you will learn to know God's will for you, which is good and pleasing and perfect
> (Romans 12:1-2, NLT).

Let's break down a few of the words that Paul uses here. In verse 1, Paul speaks of a holy sacrifice. The word "holy" is translated from the Greek word *hagios*, which means set apart by (or for) God.

The word "sacrifice" is translated from the Greek word *thusia*, which means an offering the Lord accepts because it's offered on His terms.

Paul says, "'Let God transform you into a new person.'" The word "transform" is translated from the Greek word *metamorphoó*, which, in this particular verse, means the change of moral character for the better.

So, how does God transform us? By changing the way we think—which will change our moral character.

The passage ends with Paul affirming that God's plan and purpose for us are "good and pleasing and perfect."

Romans 12:1-2 says it all. We should respond with gratitude for all that God gives us. We are to worship Him by giving our lives to Him as a living and holy sacrifice—a living and holy sacrifice that is acceptable and pleasing to Him. We are to let God transform us, to change our thinking from the ways of this world to His way of thinking—to see things the way God sees them.

As Christians, we are called to be living sacrifices in response to all God has done for us. Our focus should be on what pleases God. We are to act in accordance with His written word by offering Him a living sacrifice that is pleasing to Him. To achieve this, we must not conform to the ways of this world. We need to view this world through the lens of God. God transforms us by changing how we think, which is opposed to the world's thinking. By studying God's word, we begin to see the world through His eyes, thus changing how we think. Learn about God and His character. We must hate evil, the evils of this present world, and cling to what is good. We must hold onto the fact that our earthly lives are temporary in the big scheme of eternity. A mere vapor in the wind compared to the eternity we will spend in Heaven with our Lord and Savior.

Humility is recognition of you
in relation to God

CHAPTER 11

Humility

L et's discuss the importance of humility. The Bible contains seventy-three verses about humility, so it's essential to understand God's perspective.

What is humility? We learned in Chapter 2 that humility is the recognition of yourself in relation to God. Humility recognizes that any good thing in your life results from what God or others (sent by God) have done for you. It involves acknowledging our sins and dependence upon God's mercy and grace. In contrast, being proud involves taking credit for everything we have or have accomplished.

The humble person does not strive for position or power; they serve God and others, just like Jesus teaches in the Parable of the Wedding Feast:

> "For all those who exalt themselves will be humbled, and those who humble themselves will be exalted" (Luke 14:11, NIV).

Biblical humility involves unequivocal obedience to God's word. Humility isn't about being unassertive but having the boldness to agree with God's word in the face of opposition. True humility does not follow the masses. True humility stands on God's word, even if it's unpopular and offensive to others.

Moses is an excellent example of humility. Read about Moses in Exodus, Leviticus, Numbers, and Deuteronomy. He firmly adhered to the teachings of God and truly put others before himself. Moses was humbler than anyone else on the face of the earth (Numbers 12:3). There is so much to learn from studying this man!

Characteristics of Humility

Those with humility are aware of their spiritual bankruptcy, characterized by meekness, and characterized by living dead to themselves. Let's look more in-depth at each of these qualities.[a]

1. Aware of Spiritual Bankruptcy

The humble recognize their spiritual bankruptcy. When Jesus gave His sermon on the mount, the first thing He said was:

> "Blessed are the poor in spirit,
> For theirs is the kingdom of heaven"
> (Matthew 5:3, NKJV).

What does it mean to be poor in spirit? Recognizing our spiritual bankruptcy. Acknowledging that our sin will send us straight to Hell and that there is nothing we, in and of ourselves, can offer up to God. Recognizing that without Jesus (poor in spirit), we have no salvation and no eternal life with the Father. Notice in the passage that Jesus says, "'theirs *is*'" the kingdom of Heaven. He didn't say, "'theirs *will be*.'" The kingdom of Heaven is ours on both sides—eternally when we leave this Earth and currently when we bring a little bit of Heaven down to Earth as we build our relationship with Jesus. Charles Spurgeon, an influential Baptist preacher in England during the mid-1800s, explains poor in spirit this way: [b]

> No man ever mourns before God until he is poor in spirit! Neither does he become meek towards others till he has humble views of himself. Hungering and thirsting after righteousness are not possible to those who have high views of their own excellence.
>
> As a wise man never thinks of building up the walls of his house till he has first dug out the foundation, so no person skillful in Divine things will hope to see any of the higher virtues where poverty of spirit is absent. Till we are emptied of self we cannot be filled with God.
>
> Christ is never precious till we are poor in spirit—we must see our own needs before we can perceive His wealth. Pride blinds the eyes and sincere humility must open them or the beauties of Jesus will be forever hidden from us.

Not what I have, but what I have not, is the first point of contact between my soul and God.

To be spiritually poor is the condition of all men—to be poor in spirit, or to know our spiritual poverty is an attainment especially granted to the called and chosen!

2. Characterized by Meekness

Meekness. What do you think of when you hear the word "meek"? Webster's dictionary defines it as:[c]

Mild, deficient in spirit and courage: submissive; not violent or strong: moderate.

That could not be further from what it is. Meek, simply put, is power under control. Being meek is to exercise God's strength under His control. In Matthew 5:5, Jesus tells us, "'Blessed are the meek.'" The word "meek" is translated from the Greek word *praus*. This word describes fierce, powerful horses trained for war. The war horse was powerful but under the control of its owner.

Meekness is having the right or the power to do something but refraining for the benefit of someone else.

Jesus is the perfect embodiment of meekness. He was gentle, kind, patient, and submitted to His Father's will. Jesus could have called down a host of angels (or even just one) to wipe out those persecuting Him. He possessed that power but chose to submit to His Father's will. Jesus willingly went to the cross for our sake. Jesus is the epitome of power under control—*praus* or meek. *Strong's Concordance* states:

> Meekness is a divinely-balanced virtue that can only operate through faith.

1 Peter 3 tells us that being meek is precious to God. Many translations use the word "gentle" instead of meek. The King James Version uses the actual word "meek." 1 Peter 3:4 is an example of how different translations use "gentle" versus "meek." Yes, the King James Version can be difficult to understand, but it provides an important nuance here.

> You should clothe yourselves instead with the beauty that comes from within, the unfading beauty of a gentle and quiet spirit, which is so precious to God (1 Peter 3:4, NLT).

> But let it be the hidden man of the heart, in that which is not corruptible, even the ornament of a meek and quiet spirit, which is in the sight of God of great price (1 Peter 3:4, KJV).

So, what does it mean for us to be meek? First, we need to view the word "meek" as Jesus views it, not as the world defines it. For us, it's to be peaceful and humble and to know what is most important in life. Being meek means you follow God's word, which isn't always easy to do. It means to share God's word with others—telling others about Jesus. It means we don't brag and boast about our accomplishments (or perceived accomplishments). It means we are always sensitive to others' needs. It means we don't think too highly of ourselves but also not too lowly.

Remember, meekness isn't a weakness but an inner strength and confidence that we know who we are in God's eyes and that we are in God's hands and His Son has already won the battle on the cross where He conquered death. No matter what life throws our way, God is in our corner. We need to always remember this and keep our composure when met with opposition. Remember, meekness is power under control.

The late Reverend Billy Graham explained meekness in this way:[d]

> A strong animal like a horse or ox, able to do a great deal of work, is not "weak"—but through training is made "meek," obedient to the will of its owner. A tame horse contributes much more to life than a wild one. Energy out of control is dangerous; energy under control is powerful.
>
> That is a vivid picture of what Jesus means by "meekness." When we are apart from Christ, we are, in a sense, like a wild animal. We live according to our own desires and wishes, obeying our own instincts and ruling our own lives. But when we come to Christ our goal is different. Now we want to live for Him and do His will. This, after all, is God's will for us—to

be obedient—and He has given us His Word to help us do this.

The Bible says, "Receive with meekness the implanted word, which is able to save your souls" (James 1:21). When our lives are marked by true meekness, we will know true happiness.

3. Characterized by Living Dead to Themselves

We are to put God's will first. We are to live according to how God would have us live versus how the world would have us live. We did a deep dive into this in Chapter 10. When we give our bodies (and lives) as a living sacrifice, we are dead to self—dead to earthly desires. We are human. We live in this present world and, by human nature, we want to follow the ways of this world. However, as believers and followers of Jesus Christ, we are transformed. The Holy Spirit indwells us and helps us on our journey to become more Christlike. Being dead to self, not living according to this world, is something we have to work on daily. Some days are going to be easier than others.

———————●●———————

Humility is the recognition of you in relation to God. To be humble, we must recognize our spiritual bankruptcy; there is nothing we can offer to God for our salvation. We need to recognize how genuinely precious Jesus is. Without Him, we would spend eternity in Hell. We are to be meek, but meekness isn't a weakness; it's power under control. Exercise God's strength in your life under His control, not yours. Meekness is a divinely-balanced virtue that can only operate through faith and is so precious to God. Find true meekness, and you will know true joy. We need to be dead to ourselves and not live according to this world. Follow Jesus and put God's will first.

True success is finishing what
God sent you here to do

Don't let human knowledge
get in the way of God's wisdom

CHAPTER 12

Success

Success. Is success bad? Not if our definition of success aligns with God's definition. From an earthly standpoint, success is having money, notoriety, position, fame, or material possessions. These things are accomplishments, not true success. One can be at the top of their game and have a large bank account but can still be a failure in life and in God's eyes.

God's definition of success is realizing the promises of God and completing your divinely ordained purpose in life.[a] In other words, true success is finishing what God sent you here to do. True success offers peace of mind and joy—things that all the world's money, fortune, and fame cannot buy. True success can only be accomplished through Jesus, by following Him and having a relationship with Him.

Be Courageous

Let's examine how God directed Joshua to become successful. Joshua was an aide to Moses. He had wandered in the desert with the Israelites for forty years, and when Moses died, he took his place.

> After the death of Moses, the servant of the LORD, the LORD said to Joshua son of Nun, Moses' aide: "Moses my servant is dead. Now then, you and all these people, get ready to cross the Jordan River into the land I am about to give to them—to the Israelites. I will give you every place where you set your foot, as I promised Moses. Your territory will extend from the desert to Lebanon, and from the great river, the Euphrates—all the Hittite country— to the Mediterranean Sea in the west. No one will be able to stand against you all the days of your life. As I was with Moses, so I will be with you; I will never leave you nor forsake you. Be strong and courageous, because you will lead these people to inherit the land, I swore to their ancestors to give them"
> (Joshua 1:1-6, NIV).

The first thing that God tells Joshua is, "'Moses, my servant, is dead. Now then'" (Joshua 1:1). We first need to kill the past figuratively. Moses is dead. We cannot let yesterday hinder our tomorrow. The past is the past. Now, move forward. So often we live in yesterday or yesteryear. Sometimes, it's hard to stop dwelling on past decisions or mistakes. Sometimes, living in the past involves relishing a past accomplishment. It's okay to reflect on the past, remember, and learn from the past, but not to live in the past. Satan steals our tomorrow by keeping us focused on the past. We absolutely must focus on God and look forward.

So, how do we do this? By aligning ourselves with God and allowing the Holy Spirit to lead us. Success does not just happen. We have to move; we have to take action on our part. In verse 3, God tells Joshua, "'I will give you every place you set your foot.'" In other words, it's there for the taking; go and get it. God has already worked out our success; we must go get it. If Joshua had not crossed the Jordan as God directed, he would not have realized that God had already gone ahead of him. Joshua had to have faith to act and to move. We, too, must have faith to move as God guides our paths.

The Israelites should have entered the Promised Land forty years earlier. God was ready to give it to them; He had gone ahead of them and had worked all things out. They just had to go get it. Because they didn't trust God and move as He directed, God had them wander for forty years in the wilderness. What happens in the wilderness? Spiritual development.

We all will go through times of wilderness in our lives. Is the wilderness bad? At the time, from our perspective, yes; however, in the big scheme of things, no. God grows us in the wilderness. The wilderness is where we grow closer to God, learn, and remember His character and promises. This is where our faith grows. We remain stuck in the wilderness when our faith does not grow. God gives us a promise when we are in the wilderness.

> "Forget the former things;
>   do not dwell on the past.
> See, I am doing a new thing!
>   Now it springs up; do you not perceive it?
> I am making a way in the wilderness
>   and streams in the wasteland"
> (Isaiah 43:18-19, NIV).

When we are in the wilderness, God makes a way out for each of us; we just have to follow Him out.

I like Joshua 1:5, "'No one will be able to stand against you all the days of your life.'" No one can stop you if you are operating in God's plan for you. God's will *will* be done.

In Joshua 1:6, God tells Joshua, "'Be strong and courageous.'" God encourages Joshua. God knew it would be difficult to do precisely as God was commanding Joshua to do. God knew there would be those who would rebel against the order to take the land.

God then gives Joshua further instructions:

> "Be strong and very courageous. Be careful to obey all the law my servant Moses gave you; do not turn from it to the right or to the left, that you may be successful wherever you go. Keep this Book of the Law always on your lips; meditate on it day and night, so that you may be

careful to do everything written in it. Then you
will be prosperous and successful. Have I not
commanded you? Be strong and courageous.
Do not be afraid; do not be discouraged, for
the LORD your God will be with you wherever
you go" (Joshua 1:7-9, NIV).

Be strong and very courageous. *Very* courageous. God is really
encouraging Joshua now. God tells Joshua, "'Do not turn from
it to the right or to the left'" (Joshua 1:7). What was God telling
Joshua? God was preparing Joshua for how he would take the
land. Joshua was a warrior. He led armies; he knew how to
fight and win. God would be directing Joshua to do things
that would not make sense to him on the battlefield. God tells
Joshua not to look at things (to the right or the left) other than
what He tells him. Do exactly as commanded; do not detour.

Has God ever put on your heart to do something that didn't
make sense? If so, did you do as He directed? God is telling
Joshua not to let human knowledge get in the way of God's
wisdom. That is why Joshua needed to be very courageous, not
to let what he knew from earthly experience get in the way of
God's direction. God tells Joshua to meditate on His word day
and night so that he could do everything written in it. We have
God's word, the Holy Bible. What happens when we meditate
on God's word to know and follow it? God says in Joshua 1:8,
"'Then you will be prosperous and successful.'" There it is,
straight from God: we will be successful.

In Joshua 1:9, God again encourages Joshua to be strong and
courageous. He also tells him not to be discouraged. How often

do we get discouraged when we follow God and things are not happening according to our timetable or how we think they should be? Yes, it can be discouraging and cause us to doubt. In these verses in Joshua, God tells Joshua to be strong and courageous three times. God knows this is hard; God knows this is difficult, hence the encouragement. There is so much we can all learn just in these nine verses.

Seek God's Heart

Let's look at someone else who was successful—David.

> Whatever mission Saul sent him on, David was so successful that Saul gave him a high rank in the army. This pleased all the troops, and Saul's officers as well (1 Samuel 18:5, NIV).

Why was David so successful? Scripture tells us he was a man after God's own heart.

> "After removing Saul, he made David their king. God testified concerning him: 'I have found David son of Jesse, a man after my own heart; he will do everything I want him to do'" (Acts 13:22, NIV).

What does it mean to be "'after God's own heart'"? David was far from perfect; he had many successes and many failures. What does it take for God to look at us and say we are after His heart?

1. Have Faith

First is faith in God. David had tremendous faith in God; we know this because he talked about it and, more importantly, demonstrated it. He knew God was with him and that God would deliver him. David's faith started when he was a young shepherd boy, protected from lions and bears that attacked his flock. This same faith allowed him to slay Goliath:

> But David said to Saul, "Your servant has been keeping his father's sheep. When a lion or a bear came and carried off a sheep from the flock, I went after it, struck it and rescued the sheep from its mouth. When it turned on me, I seized it by its hair, struck it and killed it. Your servant has killed both the lion and the bear; this uncircumcised Philistine will be like one of them, because he has defied the armies of the living God. The LORD who rescued me from the paw of the lion and the paw of the bear will rescue me from the hand of this Philistine."
>
> Saul said to David, "Go, and the LORD be with you" (1 Samuel 17:34-37, NIV).

2. Seek and Meditate

Secondly, to be after God's own heart, we need to earnestly seek Him and meditate on His word. David wrote many of the psalms, declaring how he loved and meditated on God's word:

I desire to do your will, my God;
   your law is within my heart
(Psalm 40:8, NIV).

May these words of my mouth and this
meditation of my heart
   be pleasing in your sight,
   Lord, my Rock and my Redeemer
(Psalm 19:14, NIV).

May my meditation be pleasing to him,
   as I rejoice in the Lord (Psalm 104:34, NIV).

When I remember You on my bed,
I meditate on You in the night watches
(Psalm 63:6, NASB).

3. Obey

While examining God's saving work in Israel's history, Paul noted that God testified that David would do everything He wanted him to do (Acts 13:22). David obeyed God. Why does God want us to be obedient? Obedience demonstrates our love and trust for God.

4. Admit Our Sin

David also sinned; he lied, committed adultery, and had Uriah, a soldier in his army, killed. What did David do when he sinned? He ultimately admitted his sin, asked for forgiveness, and repented. We all sin. We need to recognize and confess our sins before God, ask for forgiveness, and turn from that sin as David did. David also experienced consequences for his sin. Even though God forgives us of our sins, we will often face consequences for our sins while here on Earth.

Prosper

The words "success" and "prosper" are used interchangeably throughout the Bible, depending upon the translation.

> The shepherds are senseless
>   and do not inquire of the LORD;
> so they do not prosper
>   and all their flock is scattered
> (Jeremiah 10:21, NIV).

They do not prosper; they are not successful.

Joseph was also prosperous (successful). Genesis tells us:

> The LORD was with Joseph so that he prospered, and he lived in the house of his Egyptian master. When his master saw that the LORD was with him and that the LORD gave him success in everything he did (Genesis 39:2-3, NIV).

God gives us promises of prosperity and success:

> Blessed is the person who does not walk in the counsel of the wicked,
> Nor stand in the path of sinners,
> Nor sit in the seat of scoffers!
> But his delight is in the Law of the LORD,
> And on His Law he meditates day and night.

He will be like a tree planted by streams of water,
Which yields its fruit in its season,
And its leaf does not wither;
And in whatever he does, he prospers
(Psalm 1:1-3, NASB).

Followers of Jesus Christ are destined for success. Claim what God has for you; do not turn to the right or to the left lest you mess it up. Do it God's way.

Success isn't bad as long as your definition aligns with God's definition and not the world's. Success is doing what God has sent you here to do. Success offers things money cannot buy—peace of mind and joy. Our success is accomplished by following Jesus, meditating on God's word, and allowing the Holy Spirit to guide our paths. Step out in faith, even when it does not make sense, and move as God directs you; this takes courage. We should not let human knowledge get in the way of God's wisdom. We must move to get what God has for us. There will be times when we find ourselves in the wilderness. That isn't a bad thing; this is where God grows us. Remember, do not turn to the right or to the left. Have faith, seek God, and be after His heart. If you do, God will prosper you.

Encouragers see
the potential in others

CHAPTER 13

Be an Encourager

We all need encouragement. We all need to be encouragers to others. We all go through days, weeks, or seasons where life is difficult or something is weighing heavy on our hearts. Even if you're a positive person, you, too, will have days when you need encouragement. As Christians, we need to lift others up. Sometimes, we just need to be there to listen and let someone know we are there for them and will be praying for them. Sometimes, we need to point out the positive in a specific situation. It's important to remember that we can always offer encouragement and support, even to strangers. For instance, I recently had to visit the customer service desk at a large retail store. I stood in line and was met with kindness and helpfulness from the lady at the counter. When I was leaving, I thanked her for her help and told her to have a blessed day. She responded by saying that she needed to hear that. As no one else was waiting in line, I took the opportunity to talk to her and ask how she was doing. We spoke for a few minutes, and I offered her words of encouragement. Sometimes, an encouraging word can make a massive difference in someone's day.

Satan loves to discourage us. When we get discouraged, we tend to isolate ourselves from others and keep to ourselves. When this happens, Satan can put all kinds of "untruths" in our heads. Satan does not want us to be encouraged; when we are encouraged, we get a second breath, which means we, in turn, can be an encourager as well. Paul tells us to encourage and build each other up (1 Thessalonians 5:11).

The writer of Hebrews tells us to encourage Christians who have turned to sin:

> But encourage one another daily, as long as it
> is called "Today," so that none of you may be
> hardened by sin's deceitfulness
> (Hebrews 3:13, NIV).

The first part of this verse expresses an urgency "as long as it is called 'Today.'" Meaning to do it now, do it as soon as possible. Why? Because we are not promised tomorrow.

The word "hardened" is translated from the Greek word *sklérunó*, which means:

> Obstinately stubborn, resisting what God says
> is right.

The writer of Hebrews tells us to encourage other Christians away from sin so that they won't be hardened. Sin usually comes into our lives little by little, deceiving (tricking) us to believe it's okay. The problem is that as we accept sin into our lives, we begin to have a hardened heart and are deceived. It does not happen all at once; if it did, we would quickly recognize it and turn away. It comes little by little and then begins to grow. When we see this happening in other Christians, we need to encourage them away from their sin. Sometimes, sin is easier to see from the outside looking in; hence, we can see something that the person headed down the wrong road cannot see. Hopefully, we all have someone in our lives who will point out if we are starting down a path of sin that we think is okay. Every one of us is subject to inadvertently getting on this path and having a hardening of heart.

This next verse emphasizes why it's crucial for Christians to meet regularly:

> Let us think of ways to motivate one another to acts of love and good works. And let us not neglect our meeting together, as some people do, but encourage one another, especially now that the day of his return is drawing near (Hebrews 10:24-25, NLT).

Christians are to meet regularly to encourage and strengthen one another. As we come together as one body in Christ, we build relationships. Through those relationships, we learn about what is going on in each other's lives. We can recognize when someone is discouraged, depressed, or possibly getting on the wrong path. Through these relationships, we can encourage and be encouraged.

Son of Encouragement

Let's examine Barnabas, known as the "son of encouragement" in the Bible. There are many things we can learn from him.[a] When we are first introduced to Barnabas in Scripture, we learn that he was unselfish and giving:

> Joseph, a Levite from Cyprus, whom the apostles called Barnabas (which means "son of encouragement"), sold a field he owned and brought the money and put it at the apostles' feet (Acts 4:36-37, NIV).

Barnabas demonstrated his selflessness by selling a piece of land he owned and giving the proceeds to the apostles. The apostles then used the money to provide for those in need. Giving and being generous doesn't always have to be materialistic. It can be as simple as offering a kind word, a smile, or a helping hand.

A group of Christians went to Antioch to share the good news of Jesus Christ with the Greeks. Later, the church sent Barnabas to continue spreading the message. At this time, Barnabas sought out Saul, took him under his wing, and mentored him. Together, they embarked on their first mission to Antioch. During this time, Barnabas mentored Saul from being a new follower of Jesus to becoming the greatest minister in the early church. After this mission, Saul came into his own and became known as Paul. God used Barnabas to raise up Paul.

> News of this reached the church in Jerusalem, and they sent Barnabas to Antioch. When he arrived and saw what the grace of God had

done, he was glad and encouraged them all to remain true to the Lord with all their hearts. He was a good man, full of the Holy Spirit and faith, and a great number of people were brought to the Lord.

Then Barnabas went to Tarsus to look for Saul, and when he found him, he brought him to Antioch. So for a whole year Barnabas and Saul met with the church and taught great numbers of people. The disciples were called Christians first at Antioch (Acts 11:22-26, NIV).

What do these verses tell us about Barnabas as he went to Antioch? He was devoted. He was willing to go where needed. Through his devotion, he sought out Saul and poured into his life. God used Barnabas to mentor the greatest minister to the Gentiles.

Barnabas was spiritually aware of what God was doing; he could see God's grace poured out on the first Christians. We can only see the work of God in others' lives when we look outwardly and are not self-absorbed. Not only did he recognize what God was doing for the Christians at Antioch, but he was also glad. He was sincerely happy for them. Barnabas wasn't jealous and didn't get upset that God did something for someone else.

This passage tells us that Barnabas was a good man, full of the Holy Spirit. The word "good" is translated from the Greek word *kalos*, which means:

Beautiful, as an outward sign of the inward good, noble, honorable character; good, worthy, honorable, noble, and seen to be so.

Barnabas was good, and others could see that virtue in him. Do others notice a difference in you? Do they see your goodness, integrity, character, and inner beauty? Barnabas was full of the Holy Spirit; the goodness spilled forth from him. When we are full of the Holy Spirit, others will see it. They may or may not understand, but they will know we are different.

How to Be an Encourager

What does it take to be an encourager?

1. A Pure Heart

It's important to have a pure heart that cares for others. We become more aware of others' struggles when we show compassion towards them. We can only see others' struggles when we have a genuine heart for them and not when we are self-absorbed. When we sincerely want the best for others, we strive for their well-being and are not jealous.

2. Listening Skills

Truly listen to others to understand their fears, what is breaking their heart, and what circumstances they are struggling with. It's easier to encourage someone if we know why they need encouragement. We need to listen more than we talk. Don't interrupt when someone is talking; don't turn the conversation to yourself. We show that we are engaged and care when we hear what others say.

3. Empathy

Be empathetic. When we listen and show empathy, we build trust. As a result, others are more likely to listen to our encouragement. Intently listen and ask questions. Confirm what they are saying and validate their feelings. Don't be judgmental; we build trust when we listen without judging. These things show that you care and are interested in them.

We encourage based not on where the person is but where they can be. Encouragers see the potential in others. As an encourager, we see that a person's situation or state of mind can be changed. We know this because, with God, all things are possible according to His will. We need to share that with others. All these things need to be shown and voiced with a positive attitude.

If you are not a natural encourager, you can become one. Ask God for His help in this area of your life. Strive for the things presented in this chapter. Make a conscious effort. Over time, it will become natural for you.

Be an encourager to others. The discouraged tend to isolate themselves from others and become a target for Satan. Take the time to encourage others; something as simple as a smile or kind word can brighten someone's day. Be the person people want to be around. As we encourage and lift up others, that encourages us as well. Some need encouragement to move away from sin. You never know how you may impact someone's life. Look at Barnabus; he encouraged and mentored the greatest minister of the early church. Have a pure heart as you encourage; people will notice. You will gain trust as you listen and empathize with them in their discouragement. For someone to heed your encouragement, they must trust you. Allow the Holy Spirit to spill forth from your life. Whether others understand it or not, they will take notice and see that you are different.

Every day, sweep your dirt

CHAPTER 14

Sweep Your Dirt

Remember the woman sweeping her dirt? We all have dirt in our lives. So, what is your dirt? What is it in your life, your dirt, that you need to appreciate, take care of, take ownership of, and nurture? We need to be thankful for all that God has blessed us with. Whether it's those things that money cannot buy or even our material possessions, focus on Jesus and the good in your life.

There were many topics discussed in this book that allowed us to reflect. We explored the Bible's teachings on the importance of a grateful heart and appreciating all the blessings God has bestowed upon us. It's crucial to find the good even in situations that are not so favorable. On this Earth, ruled by Satan, there will always be struggles, heartaches, hurts, and disappointments. Remember, we don't have to be of this world; we only have to live here temporarily. The song "Wonderful Life" by Matthew West[a] encapsulates this sentiment perfectly when it says, "This life ain't always wonderful, but this life ain't all there is."

This book highlights things God dislikes, which can trap us, such as materialism, comparison, pride, busyness, and grumbling. Pointing out these areas isn't intended to discourage or criticize. Instead, it's to point out things to be aware of that can gradually steal our joy when we don't even realize it's happening. Areas in our lives that can hinder our relationships and put a wedge between us and God. As that wedge grows more extensive and profound, we lose our joy, and we lose our peace. Therefore, we must be vigilant, open our eyes, and evaluate ourselves. Whether in the past, the present, or the future, we all know what it's like to stumble into behaviors and mindsets that are detrimental to us and pull our focus off of Jesus. We are human; we have imperfect bodies and need to see, realize, and recognize these flaws. Once we do, with God's help, we can work through them. Let us pray and ask God to reveal where we are lacking or have fallen into behaviors that displease Him. We can ask God to show us and help us escape these traps.

Remember to sweep your dirt, be grateful for it, and always find the good in all things. Take care of the precious things that life has to offer. Have a grateful heart and follow the example of that beautiful woman in Africa who swept her dirt.

Sweep your dirt every day; every single day, sweep your dirt.

Acknowledgments

First and foremost, I want to thank my husband, Charles—the love of my life—for always being there and being my biggest cheerleader.

To my parents, William Randall and Rita Joy Hudson, for demonstrating hard work, honesty, and integrity. For loving me unconditionally and teaching me to love Jesus.

To my daughter, Taylor, for always being upbeat and encouraging. You are the light in my life.

To my sister, Ranette, for always being someone I can look to and look up to.

To my dear friends, Cindy and Debby, for their much-needed encouragement.

Notes

Chapter 2

a. "Trichotomy vs. dichotomy of man—which view is correct?". (n.d.). Retrieved January 26, 2024, from https://www.gotquestions.org/trichotomy-dichotomy.html

b. Davis, A. (March 31, 2013). Body, Soul, and Spirit – Explained. Retrieved from https://bibleofgod.org/body-soul-and-spirit-explained/

c. Evans, Dr. T. (2022 May 31). The Concept of Truth [Sermon audio recording]. https://go.tonyevans.org/tony-evans-sermons/the-concept-of-truth

d. Evans, Dr. T. (2022 May 31). The Concept of Truth [Sermon audio recording]. https://go.tonyevans.org/tony-evans-sermons/the-concept-of-truth

Chapter 3

a. Evans, Dr. T. (2022 August 12). Putting on the Armor, Part 2 [Sermon audio recording]. https://go.tonyevans.org/tony-evans-sermons/putting-on-the-armor-part-1-1-2

Chapter 4

a. Jeffress, Dr. R. (2021 April 18). Count Blessings Not Sheep [Sermon audio recording]. https://ptv.org/broadcast-video/count-blessings-not-sheep/

b. Brown, G. (2016). 18. Living a Life of Wisdom Instead of Foolishness. Retrieved from https://bible.org/seriespage/18-living-life-wisdom-instead-foolishness

c. "What happens if God calls your name twice?" (July 20, 2020). Retrieved March 14, 2022, from https://www.christthekingkirk.org/blog/2020/7/20/what-happens-if-god-calls-your-name-twice

Chapter 5

a. Jeffress, Dr. R. (2021 April 18). Count Blessings Not Sheep [Sermon audio recording]. https://ptv.org/broadcast-video/count-blessings-not-sheep/

b. Higgins, W. (August 18, 2015). Be faithful in the little things. Luke 16:10. Retrieved from https://williamshiggins.net/2015/08/18/be-faithful-in-the-little-things-luke-1610/

c. Sang, R. (August 16, 2018). Ant-Man And 7 Biblical Ways To Avoid The Comparison Trap. Retrieved from https://drawingontheword.com/ant-man-and-7-biblical-ways-to-avoid-the-comparison-trap/

Chapter 7

a. "pride." Merriam-Webster.com. 2023. https://www.merriam-webster.com (October 30, 2023).

b. Rhodes, R. (September 3, 2023). How Did Lucifer Fall and Become Satan? Retrieved from https://www.christianity.com/wiki/angels-and-demons/how-did-lucifer-fall-and-become-satan-11557519.html

c. "When were Obadiah's prophecies against Edom fulfilled (Obadiah 1:18-20)?". (n.d.). Retrieved April 18, 2023, from https://www.gotquestions.org/prophecies-against-Edom.html.

d. Edwards, J. (n.d.). Undetected Spiritual Pride, One Cause of Failure in Times of Great Revival. Retrieved October 10, 2022, from https://www.angelfire.com/va/sovereigngrace/undetected.html

Chapter 8

a. "thorn." Encyclopedia.com. 2018. https://www.encyclopedia.com/plants-and-animals/botany/botany-general/thorn#:~:text=thorn%20%2F%20%5Bunvoicedth%5D%C3%B4rn%20%2F%20%E2%80%A2%20n.%201.%20a,become%20a%20thorn%20in%20renewing%20the%20peace%20talks. (October 30, 2023).

b. Gehrig, Lou. (2019, June 23). In Wikipedia. https://en.wikipedia.org/wiki/Lou_Gehrig

c. "Gehrig, Lou, Farewell to Baseball Address, delivered July 4, 1939, Yankee Stadium, New York" (July 2, 2020). Retrieved from https://www.americanrhetoric.com/speeches/lougehrigfarewelltobaseball.htm

d. Spurgeon, C. H. (1876, April 2). Strengthening Words from the Saviour's Lips. Retrieved from https://www.spurgeon.org/resource-library/sermons/strengthening-words-from-the-saviours-lips/#flipbook/

e.   "My Grace Is Sufficient for You: A Study on 2 Corinthians 12". (n.d.). Retrieved May 14, 2023 from https://www.bible.com/reading-plans/33036-my-grace-is-sufficient-for-you-a-study-on-2/day/5

f.   Tafone, E. (n.d.). The Big Question: Why Does God Give Us Thorns? Retrieved June 1, 2023 from https://guideposts.org/angels-and-miracles/miracles/gods-grace/the-big-question-why-does-god-give-us-thorns/

Chapter 9

a.   Jacqueline. (2016, November 6). Betsie and the Fleas: True Story of Courage and Thankfulness in Trial. Retrieved from https://deeprootsathome.com/betsie-and-the-fleas/

b.   Popova, M. (n.d.). Viktor Frankl on the Human Search for Meaning. Retrieved November 28, 2022, from https://www.themarginalian.org/2013/03/26/viktor-frankl-mans-search-for-meaning/

c.   Mayo Clinic. (n.d.). Positive thinking: Stop negative self-talk to reduce stress; The Benefits of Positive Thinking. Retrieved on December 6, 2022, from https://www.mayoclinic.org/healthy-lifestyle/stress-management/in-depth/positive-thinking/art-20043950

Chapter 10

a. "disciple." Merriam-Webster.com. 2023. https://www.merriam-webster.com (October 30, 2023).

b. Evans, Dr. T. (2022 May 19). Calling Kingdom Disciples [Sermon audio recording]. https://go.tonyevans.org/tony-evans-sermons/calling-kingdom-disciples

Chapter 11

a. Jeffress, Dr. R. (2020 March 15). Survival Tip #7: Beware of Celebrating the Summit [Sermon audio recording]. https://ptv.org/broadcast-video/survival-tip-7-beware-of-celebrating-the-summit/

b. Spurgeon, C. H. (1909, August 5). The First Beatitude. Retrieved January 6, 2023, from https://www.spurgeon.org/resource-library/sermons/the-first-beatitude/#flipbook/

c. "meek." Merriam-Webster.com. 2023. https://www.merriam-webster.com (October 30, 2023).

d. Graham Jr., W. (2019, January 1). How Can God Be Both Meek and Powerful? Retrieved from https://billygraham.org/answer/how-can-god-be-both-meek-and-powerful;

Chapter 12

a. Evans, Dr. T. (2023 February 27). The Key to Your Success, Part 1 [Sermon audio recording]. https://tonyevans.org/podcast_sermons/the-key-to-your-success-part-1/

Chapter 13

a. Price, J. (2019, May 24). Encourage the
    Encouragers. Retrieved from https://
    bibleanswer.com/encouragers.htm

Chapter 14

a. West, Matthew. (2023). Wonderful Life. On *My
    Story Your Glory* [Album]. Provident Label Group.

Dear Reader,

Thank you for taking the time to read my book. I hope you found it encouraging.

I would appreciate it if you could take a moment to share your thoughts by leaving a review on Amazon.

If you enjoyed reading this book, please consider recommending it to your family and friends.

Blessings to you and your family,

Tracy